REINHOLD NIEBUHR AND
THE ISSUES OF OUR TIME

REINHOLD NIEBUHR AND THE ISSUES OF OUR TIME

Edited and introduced

by

RICHARD HARRIES

Dean of King's College, London

MOWBRAY
LONDON & OXFORD

ISBN 0 264 67051 5

First published 1986
by A.R. Mowbray & Co. Ltd.
Saint Thomas House, Becket Street,
Oxford, OX1 1SJ

Typeset by Comersgate Art Studios, Oxford.
Printed in Great Britain by Biddles Ltd, Guildford.

British Library Cataloguing in Publication Data
Reinhold Niebuhr and the issues of our time
——————— (Mowbray's Christian studies series)
1. Niebuhr, Reinhold
I. Harries, Richard, *1936–*
230'.092'4   BX4827.NS

ISBN 0-264-67051-5

DEDICATED TO
URSULA NIEBUHR

CONTENTS

NOTES ON CONTRIBUTORS

Richard Wightman Fox is Associate Professor, History and Humanities, Reed College, Portland, Oregon. He is the author of *Reinhold Niebuhr: A Biography* (Pantheon Books, 1985) from which his essay is adapted and of *So Far Disordered in Mind: Insanity in California, 1870–1930* (University of California, 1979). He is the co-editor of *The Culture of Consumption in America: Critical Essays in American History, 1880–1980* (Pantheon, 1983).

James M. Gustafson is University Professor of Theological Ethics in the Divinity School and in the Committee on Social Thought of the University of Chicago. He is the author of *Protestant and Roman Catholic Ethics* (University of Chicago and SCM, London) and of *Ethics from a Theocentric Perspective* in 2 volumes, *Theology and Ethics* and *Ethics and Theology* (University of Chicago and Blackwells, Oxford).

Daphne Hampson is Lecturer in Divinity at the University of St Andrews. She holds a doctorate in Modern History from Oxford University, and a doctorate in Theology from Harvard University, for which her dissertation was on 'The Self's Relation to God: A Study in Faith and Love', a comparison of the structures of Lutheran and Catholic thought. She has been a teaching assistant in Theology at Harvard and a lecturer in the History of Religious Thought at the University of Stirling. She is at present writing a book on *Theology and Feminism*.

Keith Ward is Professor of the History and Philosophy of Religion at King's College, London. He has made contributions to both Moral Philosophy and Philosophy of Religion. His books include *Ethics and Christianity* (Muirhead Library of Philosophy, Allen and Unwin, 1970); *The Development of Kant's View of Ethics* (Blackwell, 1972); *Rational Theology and the Creativity of God* (Blackwell and Pilgrim Press, New York, 1982) and *The Battle for the Soul* (Hodder and Stoughton, 1985).

Ronald Preston is Emeritus Professor of Social and Pastoral Theology in the University of Manchester. He has written widely on social, political and economic matters. His most recent books are *Religion and the Persistence of Capitalism (SCM), Church and Society in the late Twentieth Century: the Economic and Political Task (SCM), Explorations in Theology – 9 (SCM)*.

Richard Harries is Dean of King's College, London. His books include *Being a Christian* (Mowbray, Oxford. Published as *What Christians Believe* in the USA, Winston Press); *Prayer and the Pursuit of Happiness* (Collins, London, and by Eerdmans in the USA). He edited with George Every and Kallistos Ware, *Seasons of the Spirit* (SPCK, London. Published as *The Time of the Spirit* by St Vladimir's Seminary Press in the USA). He has written widely on issues of war and peace and his writings in this field include *Should Christians support Guerillas?* (Lutterworth) and *Christianity and War in a Nuclear Age* (Mowbray, Oxford, forthcoming). He is currently working on an anthology of the writings of Austin Farrer for SPCK.

James F. Childress is Commonwealth Professor of Religious Studies and Professor of Medical Education at the University of Virginia. He concentrates on political ethics and biomedical ethics and has published widely in these fields including several books. He is a member of the Society of Friends.

Langdon Gilkey is Shailer Mathews Professor of Theology in the University of Chicago Divinity School. His recent books include *Reaping the Whirlwind: a Christian Interpretation of History* (Seabury, NY, 1976); *Message and Existence: An Introduction to Christian Theology* (Seabury, NY, 1977); *Society and the Sacred: Towards a Theology of Culture in Decline* (Crossroads, NY, 1981) and *Creationism on Trial: Evolution and God at Little Rock* (Winston-Seabury, Minneapolis, 1985).

Douglas John Hall holds the Chair of Christian Theology in the Faculty of Religious Studies at McGill University, Montreal. He was a student of Reinhold Niebuhr from 1953 to 1960 at Union Theological Seminary, from which he holds the Doctor of Theology degree. He is the author of several books, including *Lighten Our Darkness: Towards an Indigenous Theology of the Cross* (Philadelphia, Westminster, 1976); *Has the Church a Future?* (Philadelphia, Westminster, 1980); *The Canada Crisis* (Toronto, Anglican Book Centre, 1981); *Christian Mission: The Stewardship of Life in the Kingdom of Death* (New York, Friendship Press, 1985), etc. He is currently working on a three-volume contextual theology.

Introduction

In the realm of public affairs Reinhold Niebuhr has been the most influential theologian of our century. A whole generation of distinguished American politicians, including such people as Adlai Stevenson, Arthur Schlesinger Jr, McGeorge Bundy and Hubert Humphrey acknowledged him not only as a prime influence on their own lives but on the whole American approach to politics. 'Niebuhr is the father of us all' said George Kennan. Whilst Hans Morgenthau, himself a much respected political philosopher, wrote: 'I have always considered Reinhold Niebuhr the greatest living political philosopher of America'.

The British are less open than the Americans to the influence of theoreticians and theologians but even so Niebuhr's influence in Britain not only amongst clergy but amongst men of affairs, some of them non-believers, was remarkable. Denis Healey and Tony Benn are just two of the many who gladly acknowledge his influence on their thought. As the late Richard Crossman said '*Moral Man and Immoral Society* was one of the books which changed my life. It was the most exciting shock intellectually that I had as a young man, and I'm still recovering from it.'

Reinhold Niebuhr died in 1971 just short of his 79th birthday. A few years before he had suffered some small strokes and no doubt partly because of that his influence amongst the burgeoning theologies of the 1960s was not as massive as it had been on thinkers in the three decades previous. Moreover, as often happens when a person dies, his name and books ceased to be at the forefront of contemporary debate during the 1970s. But as all the great issues of war

1

and peace, revolution and nuclear weapons, intervention and monetarism continued to dominate the 1980s many began to feel the increasing lack of what can only be called a Niebuhrian dimension to the debates. So much of the discussion seemed, from a Christian standpoint, thin; betraying an excessive trust in purely rational, idealistic or political solutions. The depth which Niebuhr's insights brought to these perennial problems, so that the political was never seen apart from the ethical and the ethical was always coloured by fundamental considerations about the nature and destiny of man was missing. In short, the time seemed overdue for an assessment of what Niebuhr could contribute to our contemporary dilemmas, many of which he himself confronted in different forms in his own lifetime.

So in September 1984 a conference was held at King's College, London, to which nearly 150 people from Europe and North America came, a good mixture of academics and practitioners, clergy and laypeople. The conference was, I believe, worthwhile. But this book, though evoked by the conference is not simply a product of it. The importance of Niebuhr is not that he offered a system of thought valid for all time but that through reading him one comes to experience the world in a Niebuhrian way. We do not look to Niebuhr for a new *Summa theologica*. What would have delighted his heart is our ability to draw Christian insights from his writings which illuminate the dark places of political and economic life in such a way that those most actively engaged in those spheres are both chastened and encouraged; and that as a result they are guided to make wiser decisions. It therefore seemed right to produce a book which kept in mind the issues of our own time, both intellectual and practical, and which asked what light Niebuhr shed on them. The essays are not primarily concerned with what Niebuhr said in his own historical context but, on the basis of what he wrote, with the issues of our own time. With this in mind the book contains some essays specially commissioned for the purpose as well as others which had their genesis at the conference on 'Reinhold Niebuhr Reconsidered'.

Richard Fox is the author of the first full-scale biography of Niebuhr, one which is likely to be definitive for many years to come. In his chapter 'Reinhold Niebuhr – the Living of Christian realism' he examines Niebuhr's attitudes to race, nuclear weapons and the Vietnam war and shows that to the end of his life he had the 'courage to change', to use a phrase from Niebuhr's famous prayer. Christian realism, for Niebuhr, included a willingness to admit limitations in previous attitudes not only on political issues but on religious ones as well. So it was that towards the end of his life Niebuhr became increasingly appreciative of Roman Catholicism and the catholic tradition in worship, which earlier in his career he had tended to criticize as contrary to prophetic religion.

James Gustafson, who has now completed his enormously distinguished *Ethics from a Theocentric Perspective* (2 volumes) subjects the foundation of Niebuhr's thought to searching analysis. Professor Gustafson here, as elsewhere, is concerned with the relationship between Theology and Ethics. Which is prior? In what way does the one influence the other? He quotes Niebuhr: '(faith) illumines experience and is in turn validated by experience' and shows how Niebuhr's interpretation of experience in the light of Biblical faith so often proved efficacious in leading to appropriate moral and political action.

Fundamental to Niebuhr's outlook is his account of sin as pride. But is this a peculiarly male way of looking at the world? In a stimulating chapter Daphne Hampson suggests that it might be, and that as a result his understanding of human nature can be inappropriate for women. She also affirms that 'a woman's different view of the world and way of inter-relating may help to cure the human situation which Niebuhr depicts'.

For what should Christians hope? Should we look for a time when a perfect society will be established here on earth? Or should we think of each individual soul surviving death and finding fulfilment beyond space and time in heaven? Keith Ward looks at Niebuhr's teaching on this subject and argues that it is still fundamentally valid. Niebuhr's concept of, and use of, paradox, for example, is essential to the assertion of Christian truth. Professor Ward then shows that Niebuhr's view that there can be no ultimate fulfilment in the political realm yet no salvation apart from it, is rooted in the New Testament itself and the way the New Testament both negates and fulfils images of the end in the Old Testament. Niebuhr's approach, whilst it may not give detailed guidance, grounds us in an approach to the political realm that saves us from both nihilism and utopianism.

Ronald Preston heard Reinhold Niebuhr when he was a student in the 1930s and has remained a life-long admirer, student and exponent of his thought, particularly in the realm of economics. There is, argues Professor Preston, an essential tension and balance in Niebuhr's thought. However, 'Christians do not find it easy to hold to Niebuhr's subtle balance in both thought and practice'. One group that has failed to grasp or maintain the balance is the so-called 'new right'. They have sometimes claimed Niebuhr's support for policies that he himself was very far from advocating. As Ronald Preston argues, although it is essential to preserve self-regulating market forces in the economic process relative justice is more likely to be achieved through the policies of the political left than the right. The political right is not only more likely to have power on its side but the force of inertia as well.

Reinhold Niebuhr subjected the pacifism of his time to devastating criticism. Although some pacifists, notably G.C.H. Macgregor, tried to meet Niebuhr's points it is only in the last few years, with a new generation of American pacifists from a mainly Mennonite background, that pacifism has become confident again. This new wave of pacifism, which seeks to ground its outlook firmly in the New Testament, is not frightened to take issue with Niebuhr. In my essay I set out Niebuhr's own critique of pacifism and in examining his new critics try to show that, from a New Testament perspective, that is, one in which Christians live 'between the times', these critics fail to maintain the tension which is inherent in the Christian faith.

James Childress outlines Niebuhr's 'realistic-pragmatic' approach to war. He then shows that although Niebuhr rejected classical Just War thinking he used, as he was bound to use, at least one of its cardinal principles, that of proportion. And although he did not accept the immunity of noncombatants from direct attack as a moral absolute he argued on pragmatic grounds for careful, discriminate targeting. Niebuhr wrote of 'the nuclear dilemma' and did not think there was any escape from the tensions of living in a nuclear age. He was sensitive to all the aspects of that dilemma, not least the thought of what we, as moral beings, are contemplating doing to other human beings. He did, however, argue in favour of deterrence; though Professor Childress believes he was sceptical about the possibility of any just use of such weapons and was close to a 'no first use' policy – whilst at the same time being aware that it would be irresponsible to have a declaratory policy that made war more possible. In any case all the issues have to be argued out with utter realism on pragmatic grounds. There is no escape from the tension of holding to the values of both justice and peace though in our time, with the prospect of nuclear devastation, peace is the overriding priority.

Since the late 1960s Liberation Theology (and to a lesser extent the Theology of Hope) have offered a sharp critique of the traditional theological concerns of Europe and North America. The ferment caused by this, particularly in the Roman Catholic Church, is likely to continue. The Sacred Congregation for the Doctrine of the Faith at the Vatican brought forth their sympathetic but critical 'instruction' on Liberation Theology which promised a further, major study of a properly Christian Liberation Theology. Yet somehow both Liberation Theology and 'The Instruction' call out for a Niebuhrian assessment. 'The Instruction' is sound in locating and flushing out those Marxist elements which have infiltrated and distorted some current liberation theologies. Yet it lacks any Niebuhrian sense of the limitations of the rational as much as Liberation Theology itself lacks any Niebuhrian sense of the potentially demonic nature of any purely political solutions. Langdon Gilkey, who has known Niebuhr's thought well for many years, looks at his thought during his most Marxist period in the early 1930s. There he sees developing not only the familiar Niebuhrian themes about the ambiguity of power, reason and religion, but also the beginning of Niebuhr's critique of Marxism. It is there that Professor Gilkey locates the beginning of Niebuhr's emphasis on balance of power and the necessity for democratic checks. For Niebuhr was raising questions then, about his own Marxist self, that are no less pertinent today.

The denomination to which Reinhold Niebuhr belonged was not primarily Lutheran and he was critical of many of Luther's social policies. Nevertheless, as

Douglas Hall argues, no one in our century, and few before, have had such a profound grasp of Luther's theology of the cross. This *theologia crucis* however, is not for Niebuhr any more than it is for Moltmann, simply about the atonement. It is a way of looking at things which permeates all life and all theology. It enables us as it enabled Niebuhr to face life with all its tragedy, despite our own weaknesses and lack of faith. This *theologia crucis* forces us to put a large question mark against all peddlars of official optimism, whether secular or religious. But it is this same theology which enables us to affirm the world even in the face of our inclination to despair about it. Professor Hall, who himself studied under Niebuhr, argues that it is this theology that underlies both his writing on faith and his approach to the political order. He concludes by quoting Niebuhr 'The Kingdom of God must still enter the world by way of crucifixion' and adds, in a sentence true to his mentor, 'but it is the world that God's Kingdom enters, and for Christians to abandon this world is to abandon the Cross at its centre'.

RICHARD HARRIES
King's College, London
August 1985

Reinhold Niebuhr - The Living of Christian Realism

RICHARD FOX

I

A decade and a half after his death, Reinhold Niebuhr's name is still frequently invoked in moral and political debate. Conservatives and liberals both try to appropriate his stature for positions they hold dear. The conservatives look back at Niebuhr and see a Burkean defender of social order, a zealous opponent of political dreamers and do-gooders. They behold a vigorous anti-Communist polemicist who after World War Two judged the American political system of 'checks and balances' to be the epitome of good sense. Liberals and a few progressives further to the left look back at Niebuhr and see a fearless advocate of social justice, a far-seeing activist who regarded the future possibilities for social advancement as open-ended. They take heart from the example of a Christian preacher who reviled the American culture of consumption, mocked the pretensions of big business, and expressed grave doubts about the fairness and even the viability of bourgeois democracy itself.

Which is the real Niebuhr? They both are. The Socialist critique of American capitalism that he developed in the late 1920s and early 1930s gave way to an embrace of New Deal liberalism by the late 1930s. The threat of fascism, the success of Roosevelt in reforming capitalism, the machinations of the Communist Party in American leftist organizations – these and other factors led Niebuhr to revalue bourgeois democracy. By the 1950s he was a leading antagonist of the Soviets and a voluble defender of the democracy of what his friend Arthur Schlesinger called the 'vital center'. These shifts in his political views are very well known. But it is worth reflecting further upon the character of the 'Christian realism' that permitted – indeed encouraged – such shifts in political perspective and commitment. Christian realism was not a formal doctrine or even a set of positions on issues. It was a dynamic orientation towards the world, a cultivation of tension in one's apprehension of it. Christians were called, Niebuhr thought, to a life of perennial paradox: judging themselves and their world in the light of the 'eternal' or 'transcendent', working ceaselessly to transform society while resisting the illusion that society could ever be perfected. For the Christian realist there was no ultimate fulfilment in society; but neither was there any salvation apart from the life of social and political engagement.

The living of Christian realism promoted changes of opinion as the Christian constantly renegotiated the balance between taking the world as it was and demanding that it embody higher standards of justice. Before World War Two Niebuhr accentuated the quest for justice; after the war he was much more liable to accept the historic structures of Western capitalist democracy as themselves the *sine qua non* of social justice. But too much stress on that fundamental shift in his outlook tends to freeze his later years into a solid mould: he becomes an acquiescent 'Cold Warrior' who, as many 'revisionist' historians have recently argued, provided moral legitimacy for the imperial strategies that led to Vietnam. In fact Niebuhr continued in the post-World War Two period to reexamine his commitments, even though after his serious stroke in 1952 he was increasingly confined to quarters. His Christian realism provoked in him a perpetual dissatisfaction with his own political stance. This becomes clear if we look at his positions on the major public issues of the 1960s, the last decade of his life: nuclear deterrence, civil rights, and Vietnam. It is also true of his position on one major religious issue of the 1960s: the rapprochement between Catholics and Protestants. Even in his very old age Niebuhr managed to reveal the depth of his Christian realism by challenging his own earlier views – views that he believed no longer accorded with the search for justice or the life of faith.

II

One revealing clue to the nature of Christian realism is the vigorous disagreement among Christian realists themselves on concrete political issues. When they took up the question of nuclear weapons in the early 1960s they bared their differences in the pages of *Christianity and Crisis*; and Niebuhr himself shifted ground in the course of the debate. In the 1950s he had regarded nuclear deterrence with a certain equanimity. The Korean war, he thought, had shown that conflict with the Soviets would increasingly take place in small encounters fought with conventional weapons. Brushfires need not produce holocausts. He was somewhat uneasy about deterrence since it involved 'prospective guilt' – guilt that would crush any 'victorious' nation that had initiated nuclear destruction. But he perceived no alternative to deterrence in view of what he considered the perfidy of the Soviets. They were quite prepared, he thought, to intimidate Europe into political subjection; the United States must counter with its own intimidation of the Russians.

When the Russians walled off East Berlin in 1961, Niebuhr and his Christian realist colleagues debated the proper course for American policy. Some Americans

spoke of sending in American tanks to destroy
the wall, and there was general fear that a nuclear
confrontation might ensue. The realists around Niebuhr all supported the view that the United States
must retaliate if the Soviets initiated a nuclear attack.
But some suggested that nuclear weapons – 'tactical'
nuclear weapons – might have to be employed if the
Soviets were to launch a 'conventional' assault with
tanks. Niebuhr, along with his colleague John Bennett,
was shocked by the complacency of the term 'tactical'. A 'tactical' bomb was larger than the one that
devastated Hiroshima in 1945. Niebuhr wrote that 'the
first use of the nuclear weapon is morally abhorrent
and must be resisted'. His friend Kenneth Thompson
expressed his disappointment at Niebuhr's and Bennett's apparent change of heart. 'If we declare we shall
not use thermonuclear weapons except in the ultimate
defence, we have assisted the Soviet Union in plotting
a campaign of expansion and imperialism.' Carl Mayer
agreed with Thompson. He thought that Niebuhr had
helped to undermine the moral and political standpoint that 'came to be known as Christian realism'.

Niebuhr's Christian realist critics accused him of
inconsistency. In reply he pleaded guilty to the charge.
He did believe that the current balance of terror was a
condition of continued peace. But he also believed
that acquiescing in the balance of terror was unjusti-
fied. He was not tempted by nuclear pacifism, but he
did think the United States had to become more flexible about arms negotiations. It was time to abandon
'unrealistic . . . insistence on foolproof inspection',
time to 'take some risks for peace comparable to our
ever more dangerous risks in the game of deterrence'.
He and John Bennett were infusing their Christian
realism with a stronger 'idealistic' thrust than many of
their peers. Niebuhr was persuaded that the propo-
nents of first use – or of remaining silent about the

possibility of first use – were deficient in weighing 'the moral consequences of initiating the dread conflict. Could a civilization loaded with this monstrous guilt have enough moral health to survive' even if it 'won' the battle? To a close friend Niebuhr admitted that the President probably could not tie the nation's hands, but that a private citizen should be able to go on record against starting a nuclear war over Berlin. There had to be a limit to moral ambiguity somewhere, Niebuhr wrote, and this might be it. 'First use' had to be ruled out as one 'worldly' compromise that the Christian could not accept.[1]

III

After President Kennedy's assassination in November 1963, the American civil rights movement gathered political steam. President Johnson shrewdly used the sacrifice of the youthful martyr to generate a groundswell of support for his Civil Rights Bill. In the course of that campaign, Niebuhr's own views about what Gunnar Myrdal had termed the 'American dilemma' underwent a marked evolution. Civil rights had never been at the top of his list of critical issues, although he had once headed the Detroit Mayor's Inter-racial Committee. He had of course always loathed racial prejudice, and had permitted the NAACP (National Association for the Advancement of Coloured People) to add his name to the support committee of its Legal Defence Fund in 1943.

Yet he was never radical on the issue of race. When the Supreme Court decided in 1956 to ban segregated schools, Niebuhr had his doubts. He had liked the Court's 1954 decision that outlawed segregation in principle but gave the southern states time to adapt. The more uncompromising 1956 decision was 'morally right', he granted, but 'pedagogically unfortunate, for it polarized the sentiments of the south and wiped out the moderate opinion which was making real progress before the decision'. Southern whites did turn to violence in 1957 to express their opposition. Yet when Martin Luther King approached Niebuhr to add his backing to an appeal for Presidential intervention, he refused. Pressure of that sort, he wrote to Felix Frankfurter, would do more harm than good. It would appear to be a Yankee intrusion in the affairs of the south. He thought a private visit to the President by a group of southern clergymen would accomplish more.

Niebuhr persisted in pleading for an end to southern racism in the early 1960s. He was troubled by the 'closed society' of the south precisely because he was so wedded to the notion that the north was an 'open society' – and to the idea that the 'open society', one that permitted each individual to seek his or her chosen ends in freedom, accorded with the fundamental facts of human nature. 'The question', he wrote in his attack on the 'Montgomery savagery' in 1961, 'is simply whether we are prepared to treat our fellow man with the respect that his innate dignity as a human being requires and deserves'. His outcry over conditions in the south was complemented by a certain satisfaction about conditions in the north, where he assumed that 'Negroes with high talent are breaking out of the enclave in increasing numbers, thus revealing the virtue of an open society, enlarging its openness, and refuting the libel about the "innate inferiority" of their race'.

But in 1964 northern blacks became more demonstrative in their demands for equal opportunity. Niebuhr had to confront a challenge to his view of the open society – a challenge mounted in his own backyard of Harlem, which bordered Union Theological Seminary to the north. He wrote to his intimate friend Bishop William Scarlett that the Negroes were starting a boycott because of the substandard schools in Harlem. He thought they were over-playing their hands. They imagined that desegregating city schools would improve educational offerings. But such a plan would require massive bussing of white and black children outside their own neighbourhoods, and bussing would produce riots in New York as it already had elsewhere. The boycott was a tactical error, but it was a sign of the gathering Negro revolution.

He had resided on the border of the black ghetto for thirty-five years and was just now coming to appreciate the depth of the racial problem in New York. Even President Johnson's Civil Rights Bill would not suffice. In mid-1963 Niebuhr had still believed that 'there is no "increasing misery" among Negroes in this country', and therefore 'no increasingly revolutionary ardour'. But in the summer of 1964 he reversed himself. 'We are in for decades of social revolution', he wrote, because of the 'despair and hopelessness' of young northern blacks. 'The reason for this despair is obvious, and I for one was slow to gauge its import.' It was the intractability of unemployment, not the exclusion from voting booths or public accommodations. The checks and balances of the free society were not enough. The structural racism of the economic marketplace had undermined his vision of 'an open society [which] prevents revolutions by allowing all economic, racial, and cultural groups to state their claims and adjust their interests'.

In *Moral Man and Immoral Society* thirty years earlier, he had proclaimed that 'the white race in America will not admit the Negro to equal rights if it is not forced to do so'. He cautioned there against any attempt by blacks to achieve freedom through 'violent rebellion', but insisted that some kind of non-violent resistance was essential. Now he returned to the sombre realism of *Moral Man*, and vigorously supported Martin Luther King's strategy of civil disobedience. By the mid-1960s Niebuhr was strongly behind King in the latter's confrontation with 'black power' activists like Stokely Carmichael and H. Rap Brown. He did not pursue the question of how King's strategy could improve conditions for northern blacks. Tactics that worked in the south – by spurring federal action through northern moral support – might be impotent in the north, where blacks faced not blatant public indignities at drinking fountains and bus stations, but deeply rooted discrimination in jobs, housing, and schools. For the most part, Niebuhr had questions, not answers, as he contemplated the racial crisis. But it is testimony to the resilience of his Christian realism that he persisted in seeking answers, even at the cost of reconsidering one of his most cherished notions of the 1940s and 1950s: that of the 'open society'.[2]

IV

When Niebuhr's *Christianity and Crisis* decided in 1964 to break a two-decade precedent and endorse a Presidential candidate, it was partly in gratitude for President Johnson's civil rights commitment, and partly in thanks for his promise to 'seek no wider war' in Southeast Asia. At this point Niebuhr was himself of two minds about Vietnam, as he had been since the mid-1950s. On the one hand, ever since the debate about saving Chiang Kai-shek's Nationalists in the late 1940s, he had been appalled by the prospect of American military involvement in an Asian civil war. On the other hand, since the Northern Korean invasion of 1950, he was grimly determined to resist Russian or Chinese military advances in Asia. Was Vietnam a civil war or another Korea? He thought it was both. In early 1962 he observed that the Diem regime lacked political support and expressed his ambivalence. 'The loss of South Vietnam to the Communists would mean a considerable strategic loss in Southeast Asia. But . . . the loss of moral prestige through the support of an unpopular and unviable regime is also a great hazard.' Like other liberal anti-Communists, Niebuhr was stuck in a difficult dilemma. His anti-Communism persuaded him, as he put it in 1963, that 'if we withdraw the Communists will overrun the whole of Southeast Asia, including Thailand'. But his liberal convictions taught him that 'if no moral content is put into the struggle the peasants will have to choose between two police states, the one not much better than the other'. He did not imagine that Diem would become a democrat; Vietnam lacked the social basis for Western-style democracy. He did expect even an authoritarian government to be more enlightened than the family despotism of Diem and his sister-in-law Madame Nhu.

In the spring of 1965 President Johnson, despite his campaign promise, intensified the bombing of North Vietnam and began a major troop build-up in South Vietnam. At that point Niebuhr's doubts deepened. He immediately grasped that the war was unwinnable. But before moving into full-scale public opposition to American policy he had to persuade himself that the 'loss' of Vietnam was tolerable. In September 1965 he came up with a Jesuitical solution that revealed egregious misunderstanding of Southeast Asian realities but at least allowed him to begin to justify American withdrawal. 'It might be wise to persuade Thailand', he wrote, 'to offer asylum to all anti-Communist warriors, and then defend this asylum with massive military power. This would be proof of our strength as well as our sense of honour to Asia.'

Once again Christian realists split stridently on a concrete political issue. Niebuhr and Bennett began their steady march into the ranks of the 'doves'. Paul Ramsey and other 'hawks' lamented that 'even

Reinhold Niebuhr signs petitions and editorials as if Reinhold Niebuhr never existed'. The most painful moment for Niebuhr came when his old friend (from the Americans for Democratic Action) Vice President Hubert Humphrey, an exuberant backer of President Johnson's escalation, came to New York in early 1966. He was to deliver the major speech at the twenty-fifth anniversary tribute to *Christianity and Crisis*, and made use of the occasion both to praise Niebuhr's realism and to justify the war. Niebuhr was aghast at Humphrey's ebullient leap into the Vietnam quagmire, but he was also worried about his own state of mind. He was not accustomed to preaching against American military ventures.

In World War One he had been a violent critic of anti-war sentiment in his own German-American community. In World War Two and Korea he had been a highly visible advocate of American war aims. But in 1966 he had to confess to Will Scarlett that he was worried by his own lack of patriotism. He found himself taking satisfaction at the American embarrassment in Vietnam – a sentiment that surprised and consternated him. For the first time in his life he felt ashamed of his own country. His prior loyalty to the transcendent realm of God's love – a love that could take concrete social shape only, he believed, in the form of justice – led him even in his very old age (he was 74 in 1966) to re-examine one of the deepest loyalties he had ever embraced: his love of country.[3]

V

Niebuhr's readiness to shift positions as the times demanded was apparent not only in his political views, but in his religious ideas. When he published *Man's Nature and His Communities* in 1965, he titled the opening chapter 'Changing Perspectives'. It was a beautiful statement of the fundamental character of Christian realism: its refusal to rest content with any religious, moral, or political status quo, its dynamic embrace of tension and paradox as the Christian's lot in this world. There was both suffering and a measure of fulfilment in that life. The Christian could never reach a point of relaxation in the quest for justice. He or she was a Sisyphus rolling a boulder up the hill. But there was a certain contentment contained in the life of historic responsibility: the knowledge that one was in balance between the immanent possibilities and transcendent impossibilities of the love ethic, the hope that beyond the tragedy of human existence there lay a final fulfilment.

In 'Changing Perspectives' Niebuhr made clear that his Protestant faith had been gradually modified by his increasing admiration for the Catholic as well as Jewish traditions. In earlier years he had frequently lauded Catholics for their 'organic', social sensibility, which 'individualistic' Protestants often lacked. But the Catholic Church still had seemed to him basically idolatrous: worshipping Mary as well as God, placing the Pope on a super-human pedestal, regarding itself as an unerring institution. Its 'natural law' moral theory derived from the Stoics and Aristotle took insufficient account of the historically shifting character of human nature. Catholic opposition to 'artificial' birth control was one unfortunate fruit of an absolutist conception of natural law. But the principled Catholic stance on civil rights in the south in the 1950s, and his friendship with liberal Catholics like John Cogley and John Courtney Murray made him much more sympathetic. The hierarchical structure of authority in the Catholic Church permitted the bishops to discipline priests and laity alike; in the Protestant churches there was no authority to protect the parson against the prejudices of his congregation. Niebuhr thought the best com-

promise lay in Bishop Scarlett's Episcopal church,
which he had first come to appreciate when, as a
young pastor in Detroit, he got to know and love
Bishop Charles Williams.

By the mid-1960s, after Pope John XXIII's encycli-
cals *Mater et Magister* and *Pacem in Terris* and the
Second Vatican Council, Niebuhr was consistently affir-
mative about the Catholic contribution. 'It has always
been one of the virtues of Catholicism', he wrote in
1961, that it 'skipped the whole period of classical
economy and never doubted that political authority
should exercise dominance over the economic sphere
in the interest of justice'. Protestants and Catholics
could nurture one another, he wrote in 1969 in one of
his last major articles, since they shared a common
inheritance and each rightly stressed important virtues:
the Catholics unity, order, and the social dimension of
existence; the Protestants pluralism, liberty, and the
individual transcendence of community.

Niebuhr's revaluation of Catholicism did not mean
that he was coming to prefer a sacerdotal, or sacramental, view of the Church. It is true that with his own
preaching career at an end, he found it hard to abide
Protestant, pulpit-centred worship. There were not
enough good preachers. The Catholic mass, he wrote
privately in 1967, was 'in many respects more reli-
giously adequate than our Protestant worship', though
there was still 'superstitious belief in magic in the
hearts of many worshippers'. Many 'intelligent Catholics' found the mass to be 'a symbol of the mystery
which makes sense out of life'. He wished Protestants
had an equally potent symbol. His own ecclesiology,
sketchy as it was, remained fundamentally Protestant
in its stress on symbolism. There was no 'real presence' of God in the sacrament, but a symbolic repre-
sentation of God's presence. The church was a
community of grace, but grace was mediated more

through the Word that was preached than through the Eucharist that was broken and shared. Niebuhr's grace was verbal, active – a grace that confronted the believer and challenged even the Church itself. A sacramental Church was too liable to passivity, self-satisfaction, too prone to believe itself sanctified. Beginning with his Detroit pastorate Niebuhr therefore stressed the Jewish, prophetic roots of Christianity. He emphasized the role of the prophet as troubler of the worshipper's premature tranquillity. The Church was not the embodiment of God's grace or even the place where that grace was experienced; it was the place where people acknowledged their unworthiness and prayed for the fulfilment that came through self-giving instead of self-seeking. Niebuhr had a genuinely liturgical sensibility, but he restricted the expression of it to his prayers. He was afraid of offering too much reassurance, becoming too much the priest. His 30-second prayers delivered after his sermons contained a concentrated dose of mystery, emotion, and celebration. They were verbal sacraments that often reached true poetic beauty. With this prayer Niebuhr closed his sermon at St George's Episcopal Church in New York City in 1960:

Eternal God, Father Almighty, maker of heaven and earth, we worship you. Your wisdom is beyond our understanding, your power is greater than we can measure, your thoughts are above our thoughts; as high as the heaven is above the earth, your majesty judges all human majesties. Your judgement brings princes to naught, and makes the judges of the earth as vanity; for before the mountains were brought forth or ever the earth and the world were made, even from everlasting to everlasting you are God.

Give us grace to apprehend by faith the power and wisdom which lie beyond our understanding;

and in worship to feel that which we do not know, and to praise even what we do not understand; so that in the presence of your glory we may be humble, and in the knowledge of your judgement we may repent; and so in the assurance of your mercy we may rejoice and be glad.

VI

In Niebuhr's eyes religion was more a matter of trust than of belief. From his father Gustav, who was also a preacher, he had inherited – as he put it in 1965 – 'an understanding of religious faith as trust in the meaning of human existence'. True faith was 'childlike in its single-heartedness' while avoiding the 'childish belief that God is on the side of the believer'. To believe in God was not to feel oneself chosen, set apart from other human beings by some eternal favour, but to feel oneself judged. The Christian was consternated before being reassured. The genius of Niebuhr's Christian realism was its capacity to generate an active commitment to social and political action while holding that action under the sanction of divine judgement. There could be no peace for the Christian realist – only an occasional deep breath before the next in a never-ending series of re-examinations. No commitment was above challenge. No party, programme, or institution was to be spared the searing scrutiny, just as none was to be condemned without seeking out the good that might be found in it. At its best Christian realism was a distinctively modern yet identifiably traditional faith. It grasped the fundamental relativity of modern existence, the need to remain open to new experience, and the stultifying smugness of religion or piety that failed to appreciate the brokenness of human life. But it also grasped the enduring promise of historic orthodoxy, which viewed human nature as 'determined' yet still 'free' to devote itself to good or to evil in this earthly vale of tears. The Christian in Niebuhr's view was called to be in the world but not entirely of it; in that unsettling tension Christians could live lives that were, as he put it to Will Scarlett, 'full of grace and grief'.[4]

NOTES

1. Niebuhr, 'Our Moral Dilemma', *Messenger*, Nov. 5, 1957, p. 5; Niebuhr and Thompson, 'The Nuclear Dilemma: A Discussion', *Christianity and Crisis*, Nov. 13, 1961, pp. 202–203; Carl Mayer, 'Moral Issues in the Nuclear Dilemma', *Christianity and Crisis*, Mar. 19, 1962, p. 38; Niebuhr, 'Logical Consistency and the Nuclear Dilemma', *Christianity and Crisis*, Apr. 2, 1962, p. 48; Niebuhr to June Bingham, Oct. 29, 1961, Niebuhr Papers, Library of Congress, Washington, D.C.

2. Niebuhr, 'The States Rights Crisis', *New Leader*, Sept. 29, 1958, p. 7; Niebuhr to Frankfurter, Feb. 8, 1957, Frankfurter Papers, Library of Congress; Niebuhr, 'The Montgomery Savagery', *Christianity and Crisis*, Jun. 12, 1961, p. 103; Niebuhr, 'Revolution in an Open Society', *New Leader*, May 27, 1963, pp. 7–8; Niebuhr to Scarlett, Feb. 3, 1964, Niebuhr Papers; Niebuhr, 'The Struggle for Justice', *New Leader*, Jul. 6, 1964, p. 10; Niebuhr, *Moral Man and Immoral Society*, pp. 252–253.

3. Niebuhr, 'Can Democracy Work?', *New Leader*, May 28, 1962, p. 9; Niebuhr, 'The Problem of South Vietnam', *Christianity and Crisis*, Aug. 5, 1963, p. 143; Niebuhr, 'Consensus at the Price of Flexibility', *New Leader*, Sept. 27, 1965, p. 20; Paul Ramsey quoted in John Bennett, 'From Supporter of War in 1941 to Critic in 1966', *Christianity and Crisis*, Feb. 21, 1966, p. 13.

4. Niebuhr, 'Mater et Magister', *Christianity and Crisis*, Aug. 7, 1961, p. 142; Niebuhr, 'Toward New Intra-Christian Endeavors', *Christian Century*, Dec. 31, 1969, pp. 1663–1667; Niebuhr, 'From the Sidelines', edited version published in *Christian Century*, Dec. 19–26, 1984, p. 1197; Niebuhr, *Justice and Mercy*, ed. Ursula M. Niebuhr, New York, 1974, p. 37; Niebuhr, 'Some Things I Have Learned', *Saturday Review*, Nov. 6, 1965, p. 63.

Theology in the Service of Ethics: An Interpretation of Reinhold Niebuhr's Theological Ethics

JAMES GUSTAFSON

I. *Introduction*

Every theologian who attends self-consciously to ethics attempts to establish some coherence between what he or she writes in primarily theological terms with what is written in primarily ethical terms. Every ethician who attends self-consciously to theology also seeks coherence between the two realms of discourse. The systematic question that grounds this study of Reinhold Niebuhr is this: Ought the theological concepts and views determine what is written about ethics? Or is it proper for the ethical concepts and views to determine what is written about theology?

Before developing my interpretation of Niebuhr's thought, I shall develop some comparisons and distinctions which provide a context for my analysis.

First, we have clear examples in Western ethics of authors who take polar opposite positions on the systematic question. The normative supremacy and dominance of the theological is central to the ethics of Karl Barth. In his case both the form and the content of ethics follow coherently from his doctrine of God, which includes the ways in which God is related to human beings and to the world. It is the doctrine of God that first must be developed and defended, Barth claims, and ethics is part of and follows from the doctrine of God.

The normative supremacy and dominance of the ethical over the theological is central to the moral philosophy of Kant. The very need to say something about God is based upon the way in which ethics is developed. What Kant says about God is a postulate of the pure practical reason; human beings cannot have a knowledge of God on which to base, and from which to develop, moral values and principles.

Many writers have not declared themselves as forthrightly on this issue as have Barth and Kant. There are ways of writing theological ethics that avoid a clear decision about which is in the service of the other; theologians call this procedure a dialectical relation between ethics and theology. I remain convinced, however, that in any coherent and comprehensive theological ethics there is, if not a clear and defended choice, a weight or preference. This weight, if it does not determine the form and content totally, makes a difference at critical points in the development of a position.

Second, every writer of theological ethics, no matter 2. what he or she decides about the first issue, finds certain theological themes to be more important than others. The selection of theological themes and the ways in which they are used coheres with the form and the content of the ethics. I shall briefly illustrate this.

For some writers the doctrine of God is the primary point of theological attention. What is said about God and about how God is related to the world makes a difference in ethics. For Barth the graciousness of God is the ultimate thing to be said, his use of analogies from relationships (covenant, speaking and hearing, etc.) determines the form of the ethics that follow from the doctrine of God. The historic contrast to this is the use of the analogy of being which theologically backs the ethics of natural law. That resulted in a marked emphasis upon continuities of principles and values, made possible an ethic of virtue and provided a basis for a casuistry that is not possible in Barth's theology and ethics.

The idea that God is active in history leads to an ethics of response to God's action; this is quite different from the ethics that cohere with God as simply a principle of transcendence or with God as an ordered being in which all other beings participate. Or, if the Christian view of God is deemed to be that God is (virtually if not totally) love, love becomes the central concept of Christian ethics. How one relates to the theme of love differs depending on choices made about ethics: love can be an ideal to be approximated, a principle or rule to be applied, a motive to be acted out, or a pattern of relations to which behaviour ought to conform.

For some writers theological anthropology is more central. How the theological anthropology is developed (both in form and content) affects the ethics. At least there has to be coherence between them, no matter which (theology or ethics) is deemed decisive. There is normally coherence between an author's ethical writings and his or her weight of emphasis on man as sinner, or as justified sinner, or as renewed and directed by sanctifying grace. There is normally coherence between how the human person is understood and both the theology and the ethics; it is not possible to develop an ethic of virtue as one has it in classic Catholic theology on the basis of the radical existentialist view of freedom that one finds in some modern continental theology.

We have seen in recent decades the resurgence of theological ethics for which eschatology is the central doctrine. What one says about eschatology makes a difference to the ethics that cohere with it. For example, it is harder to define proximate ends and regulatory action guides from an eschatology that anticipates

a radical newness (a future coming toward the present) than it is an eschatology that sees the end to be
the fulfilment of the creation. An eschatology that
dares to find human values correlative to the vision of
the end, such as one found in American social gospel
writers, will sustain a different ethic from a more dra-
matic open future view. If the Kingdom of God is a
Kingdom of love, love in turn backs co-operativeness,
and co-operativeness in turn backs socialization of
institutions including the economic ones, etc.

Thus, when one analyses theological ethics one
looks not only for whether ethics is in the service of
theology (or vice versa), but also for the theological
themes or doctrines that ascend in importance in the
position. One also looks to see how these themes or
doctrines function ethically. Do they function as myths
or symbols to interpret history and the more particular
circumstance in which action takes place? Thus, do
they have heuristic power to disclose 'reality' and in
the light of this disclosure one can make more rational
choices? Do they function as the ground of moral
norms and principles which become action guides in
the conduct of human affairs? Do they back certain
ideal ends to be approximated? The general point is
this: which theological theme is most important to the
moral theologian will affect the ethics; vice versa, if
the ethics is determinative it will predispose the theologian to select certain theological themes.

Third, every writer of theological ethics draws on 3.
various *sources* for his or her work; one can examine
which sources are used, what authority each seems to
have, and whether one source or another dominates.
We are familiar with certain Protestant emphases on
scripture alone; theology and thus theological ethics is
to be based upon exegesis. We are also familiar with
the ways in which choices are made about what parts
of the Bible, or what bibical themes, are central: the

exodus narrative, the eighth century prophets, the teachings of Jesus, or the Pauline views of justification each affect ways in which ethics is worked out. Metaphysical sources have been used: the Neo-platonic pattern of Augustine's ethics forms it decisively; the combination of the Neo-platonic and the Aristotelian elements in Thomistic ethics affects it crucially. (Whether the metaphysics is in the service of the biblical, or vice versa, thrusts this issue back to our major systematic question.) We have had appeals to common human experience as a source; it was common for Puritan theologians, for example, to develop arguments from experience (with philosophic sophistication – not merely observations) and then to show how arguments from the Bible led to the same or similar conclusions while being sure that the biblical basis was the more certain authority.

I shall not enumerate more sources since it is my intention only to call attention to the issue of the sources. How they are used, and how they are related to each other, is important, for choices about this affect the development of the ethics.

4. The fourth and final aspect of the context of my analysis pertains to the 'types' of ethics that the theologian develops, adopts or adapts. Analyses of Western ethics have long noted the distinction between *Tugendlehre* (ethics of virtue), *Phlichtenlehre* (ethics of duty), and *Gutenlehre* (ethics of value or the good). We have the Weberian distinction between ethics of conscience and ethics of cultural and social responsibility: the former is more deontic and the latter more consequentialist. We have H. Richard Niebuhr's proposal for an ethic of responsibility or *cathekontic* ethics. If the theologian adopts the language of ideals, certain things follow: one approximates or realizes ideals, or one compromises the ideal in relation to the historically possible. If one argues that biblical ethics

are deontic, as Paul Ramsey does, and that one is to work out ethics in the biblical mode, one establishes an ethic of principles and rules and procedures for their application. We have ethics of witness, or attestation, or reflection in the work of Barth; man is to witness to, attest to, reflect, and confirm the good which is God's grace; procedurally we are left with something like a focused intuition in the moment of choice guided by 'points to be considered'. And certainly theologians have mixed theories of ethics, something they have a right to unless moral philosophers are to determine the canons of judgement about theological ethics. They can always take recourse, if they have mixed theories, to the variety of moral discourse in the Bible and the fact that biblical ethics does not have a consistent theory that fits distinctions made by moral philosophers.

It is worth examining whether there is coherence between the ethics and the theology of any given author precisely on this point. Does a particular doctrine of God, for example, back a particular 'type' of ethics? For example, H. Richard Niebuhr's view of God acting in all actions upon us seems to require his ethics of response and responsibility. Or does one decide what ethical theory is correct, and fit the theology into it? Or does one, somewhat pragmatically, have mixtures of ethical theory?

I have developed these comparisons and distinctions because they set a context for my analysis of Reinhold Niebuhr's theological ethics. My intention in what follows is to give a critical analysis of his writings in the light of this introduction. My aspiration is that this analysis will elucidate features of his theological ethics, and thus expand our understanding of it. One's own external critical response to his work depends upon one's own judgement about items I have elaborated in this introduction.

II. *An* ETHICAL *Profile of Niebuhr's Theological Ethics*

Reinhold Niebuhr's interests were primarily in the arena of morality and politics in contrast to systematic theology; this is unassailable. Whether one examines the course of his writing from the earliest onwards, or whether one looks at the topics that attracted his attention in almost any particular writings, it is clear that his motivating interest was to address matters of morality and politics. One finds almost no developed systematic attention, for example, to the Trinity or to salvation of individuals and of the world as one does in the thought of most historic Christian theologians. And in the sphere of the moral his concentration was on the social aspects of life, and here primarily on institutionalized social aspects – politics, international affairs, and economics. He does not write about lying.

It is my intention to delineate an ethical profile of Niebuhr's writings. I shall follow roughly what I have called the four base points of theological ethics.

First, theological ethics, like other ethics, has to account for the procedures used to come to a practical moral or social choice. Niebuhr was not methodologically self-conscious in the way that many more recent theologians have become. One looks in vain for a specific articulation of his 'method' of practical reasoning. To form a profile of his method of making practical judgements requires that one draw inferences from his actual practice. The fairest general characterization is that Niebuhr had, from the perspective of philosophically developed ethical theories, a mixed method, with the weight on the assessment of probable consequences of alternative courses of action. If one takes the Weberian distinction between an ethic of conscience and an ethic of cultural or social responsibility, it is clear that Niebuhr's work fits the latter type. Indeed, his polemic against Christian pacifism was in large part an attack on its failure to take the prudential calculations required to assess probable social and political outcomes of the position. Prudential calculations were for Niebuhr a large part of ethics; this distinguishes his work from strict deontic ethics. It is clear that he was not worried about committing the 'naturalistic fallacy'; if one was not to maximize what could be deemed to be good consequences, one surely was to minimize those deemed to be evil. How the distinction between fact and value, between the is and the ought (or ought to be), was to be dealt with as either a logical or a moral problem was not a matter that attracted his attention. But how he came to his assessment of states of affairs that ought to be altered, or of moral judge-ments of probable consequences, was not merely a matter of affective intuiting. Norms and values directed his judgements, and the framework in which he used them is complex. One aspect of his procedure was the interpretation of events and circumstances, indeed, the interpretation of history itself; to this I will attend below.

Here I shall concentrate on two distinguishable types of moral language that Niebuhr used to provide direction for action, the language of a moral ideal, and the language of law. I think it did not occur to him that the intermingling of these two created problems or even tensions. For him any tension was resolved by stating that the law of love was an ideal.

The tension I wish to note is between the different ways in which reflection about these two terms nor-mally works; both are used in Niebuhr's work. Ideals are ends' language; one approximates or realizes ideals, or one compromises the ideals to be actually effective. The contrast is to the actual, and the moral problem is the distance between the ideal and the actual or, in language Niebuhr often uses, between the transcendent and the historical. To follow out this pat-tern one normally gives quite specific content to the ideal, and one calculates the means by which the ideal can be most closely approximated or most fully realized. This kind of language is present in Niebuhr's work, but for him the ideal was not so much an end as something in the light of which the actual was judged. It does not exclude the use of the language of law. Love is the ideal, but love is also the law.

The language of law functions differently. One is to comply with law, whether it is grounded in the order of nature, in a positive civic legal system, or in a revelation. The authority of law is normally construed to be different from that of ideals. One applies law to cases, both antecendently to action to direct conduct and retrospectively to judge its rightness.

Niebuhr writes over and over about love as 'the law of life'. This law of life is harmony. This seems to be a statement about Being; although it is not explicated as such, it echoes Augustine's view that all things are created to be in harmonious relations to each other. For Augustine the practical implications of this are an ethic of relations of things to each other in their proper proportions so that they more perfectly manifest the intended harmony of their createdness. There is an implied ethic of right relations of persons, things and institutions, etc., to each other in Niebuhr, but it is not prominent in his moral language. And surely Niebuhr does not use harmony as the ontological moral ground from which one develops practical principles in the manner of classic natural law theory. I think harmony functions as a transcendent 'ideal' (to be sure, ontologically grounded) in the light of which the 'actual' is critically interpreted; it is not a basis from which principles of action are inferred.

Love is for Niebuhr not only harmony, but a norm of sacrificial giving for the sake of others. It is also, then, law in another sense. How he does *not* work out the use of this norm is instructive. A comparison with the work of Paul Ramsey makes my point. For Ramsey *agape* is a revealed norm of life which is no more immediately applicable to political and social affairs than it is for Niebuhr, but the practical task of ethics is the 'in-principling' of *agape* in rules which then are rationally and casuistically applied to particular circumstances and cases. Just-war theory for Ramsey is love 'in principles', for example; it is an 'in-principled' application of *agape*. Ramsey's procedure reduces, and for some critics eliminates, the tension between the norm of love and the conduct of persons and institutions. Love as *agape* for Niebuhr is not a law applied to cases through secondary principles; for him this procedure would reduce the starkness of the tension, and thus the sense of judgement under which persons, institutions, and history stand. By seeing values or principles such as justice not as rational derivatives for the application of love, but as principles dialectically related to a transcendent law of love, Niebuhr sharpens contrasts. But the dialectical relation has procedural consequences; it does not back refined casuistic procedures that Ramsey's view does and perhaps leaves judgements open to a more intuitive resolution. At least they come more from assessment of potential consequences than from directive restraints of moral rules. It is notable, for instance, that in his writings about war Niebuhr does not attend to and use the principles of the just-war tradition in any highly developed way.

The term justice functions importantly in Niebuhr's ethics; it is basically a principle of equality. But Niebuhr certainly does not develop a theory of justice, nor does he explicate his use of the term in relation to classical or contemporary literature written by philosophers. For example, one gets no precise discussion of 'equals shall be treated equally' that calls for elaboration of who the equals are (persons, nations, social groups), or of the principle by which they are to be determined as equals (need, merit, etc.). The idea of justice informs prudential judgements; the tension between it and the transcendent ideal is always stressed. It is not, however, used to describe some historical ideal state of affairs to be approximated nor is it developed as a basis for refined rational application in casuistry. To say it is 'love applied' would not fit Niebuhr's thought accurately, for that would mitigate the moral tension so central to his life and thought.

In my judgement the dominant overarching moral frame of reference in Niebuhr can be stated in terms of the tension between the ideal and the actual. This backs very different ethical outworkings from other theologians; for example, from the ethics of responding to God's humanizing activity in the world (Paul Lehmann), the ethics of attesting to the reality of the good (Barth), or the ethics of natural law. In this respect I think Niebuhr was very much an heir of the liberal Protestant social gospel tradition. But some comments about Niebuhr's procedures for assessing probable consequences of alternative courses of action are required.

Fundamental to this was the interpretation of events in the light of certain symbols; before turning to this, however, other observations are in order. Although 'cost-benefit analysis', game theory, and other procedures that policy analysts now use had not been developed as they have since his time, there were more 'scientific' efforts to engage in prediction or forecasting of consequences that he used. He did not use more technical literature from social and policy sciences as is now frequently seen in Christian social ethics in at least North America, for example, in the Bishops' *Pastoral Letter on War and Peace*. Certainly his assessment was illuminated by his use of the term justice, and others. Certainly he drew historical analogies; one recalls the frequency with which he calls attention to the perversion of the ideals of the Bolshevik Revolution in the era of Stalinism to show how moral and social ideals are corrupted by power. But one does not find in his work specific attention to the philosophical issues raised by critics of the ethics of consequences, particular in its utilitarian form. Nor does one find formulations of very precise policy proposals and the development of the steps or means by which they could be executed. His canvas was larger and he painted in broader strokes.

To a subsequent generation of moral theologians in North America Niebuhr's lack of methodological self-consciousness about practical reason sometimes appears to be philosophically naive. Perhaps Paul Ramsey had Niebuhr in mind when he wrote that Protestant social ethics was roaming 'in the wastelands of utility'. If the lacuna is to be judged an intellectually culpable lapse, what accounts for the effectiveness of Niebuhr's writings among both religious and secular groups? Perhaps he was a very learned 'moral virtuoso' whose brilliance achieved more intuitively what less talented minds have to strive toward more methodically.

The second base point of theological ethics is what I call the interpretation of circumstances. Every ethician makes judgements about what circumstances are morally relevant to the problem at hand; how inclusive or exclusive they are depends upon other choices. One choice is about ethics itself; for example utilitarians include far more than strict Kantians. Another is the scope of explanation of how the circumstances addressed have come to be; for example, a psychoanalytic interpretation of events in the light of the characteristics of a powerful agent will be quite different from that of an institutional historian or analyst. The symbols, myths, concepts or principles used to explain the problem at hand determine to a great extent the recommended or prescribed courses of action to rectify it. An economic analysis of a social issue leads to a basically economic solution.

At this point one finds more theory in Niebuhr's writings, i.e., his theory of myths. In my judgement his effectiveness rested heavily on the persuasiveness of his interpretation of historic events and movements. They unmasked deceptions and illusions, and exposed what he often called 'reality'. The persuasiveness of his analyses disposed persons to take seriously his proposed recommendations. His theory of myths supported this aspect of his work; his appropriation of how they provide insight into reality is consciously developed. The 'truth' of revelation was not so much a correlation between religious language and the being and acts of God as its power to disclose profound dimensions of human experience. Revelation is heuristic in function and its 'truth' is confirmed by what it unveils about human life. Many examples can be cited; I select only one.

> Most profoundly the atonement of Christ is a revelation of what life actually is. It is tragic from the standpoint of human striving. . . . Yet this crucifixion becomes the revelation of that in human history which transcends human striving. . . . Without the cross men are beguiled by what is good in human existence into a false optimism and by what is tragic into despair. The message of the Son of God who dies upon the cross, of a God who transcends history and is yet in history, who condemns and judges sin and yet suffers with and for the sinner, this message is the truth about life.[1]

'[Faith] illumines experience and is in turn validated by experience.'[2] This truth about life is morally, socially, and politically relevant. Indeed, I think one can make a case that Niebuhr came to his interpretation and use of crucial Christian myths and doctrines through his polemics against other uses of them (e.g., Protestant liberalism and Protestant orthodoxy) by assessing the moral and social consequences of other views. The errors of Protestant liberalism led to illusions about 'reality' which in turn led to political and social consequences that were, from Niebuhr's standpoint, evil. My illustration is his statement about the atonement; it can readily be substantiated that he said similar things about other Christian doctrines or myths and used them in similar ways.

The importance of the assurance of the Kingdom of God coming at the end of history is that the belief assures hope, and thus Christianity does not lead to a finally tragic view of life. Such a view of life could lead to despair; despair could lead to passivity; passivity could contribute to the flourishing of evil. The importance of the idea of sin, which he expounded with a brilliance that has seldom been equalled in the history of Christian thought, is its revelatory power to expose the deepest propensities of individuals and collectivities; indeed, the idea of sin had predictive powers so that courses of events could be anticipated in its light. Christian doctrines, or myths, reveal the reality of mercy; this belief frees persons and communities to live and act prudentially and without the self-deception that could lead to assuming that their actions were the unambiguously right ones for all times. The idea of God, itself, functions as a principle of transcendance which relativizes and yet judges the temporal and the historical; events can be interpreted in the light of this transcendence in such a way that persons and nations recognize that the historically possible never achieves the transcendently ideal and thus is always under judgement.

Certainly Niebuhr's selection and development of

theological symbols coheres with his ethical and political thought. <u>Theology is more in the service of ethics,</u> I <u>believe than ethics is in the service of theology</u>. Brief contrasts with other authors support this judgement. He does not develop his doctrine of God and claim it has authority because it is biblical, and on the basis of that authority use it ethically, as Barth did. Nor would the choice that his brother made to adopt the idea of God acting in history provide backing for the kind of interpretation of events and ethics that he developed. Moltmann's ethical use of eschatology is quite different from Reinhold Niebuhr's, and issues in differences in the ethics of the two. Niebuhr did not use the exodus event as a crucial myth for interpreting history, and the political ethics of liberation theologians who do is different from his as a selection and use of theological symbols to interpret events and the patterns of ethics. For most, if not all of them, however, the justification for the 'truth' of the symbols is not (at least not as forthrightly as Niebuhr's) that they 'reveal what life actually is' so that one can avoid the evils that endanger social and political life.

3.   The third base point of theological ethics is <u>anthropology</u>; I believe all ethical theory is based in large part on a descriptive anthropology. How a thinker describes human beings determines to a considerable extent how he or she will interpret morality and prescribe right actions. I suppose two components are present in every description of persons as moral agents: voluntariness and purposiveness.[3] Without some measure of self-determination there could be no moral accountability, and without some ends or purposes (if only the purpose of acting rationally) there would be no direction to human activity. But how ethical thinkers specify the range of self-determination and their specification of how purposes are formed makes a difference to their ethics. And, I believe, how a thinker describes humans

as agents has crucial implications of his or her normative thinking. The descriptive anthropology of a socio-
biologist or a Freudian backs a different view of ethics
from that of Kant or Augustine.

I think that few will disagree with the judgement that
Niebuhr's work on man is his most systematic, most
precisely developed, most learned, and most lasting in
its significance. From the earliest writings his occupa-
tion with a proper understanding of what human
beings are and are not capable of, what their illusions
and self-deceptions are, what their possibilities and
limits are, and what the effects of their collectivities
are is most notable. In my judgement one sees a progressive development of insight from the relatively
simple moralism of some of the early writings to the
learning and profundity of the Gifford Lectures. The
gap between the ideal and the actual gets increasingly
a sophisticated explanation. Indeed, one can adduce a
considerable amount of evidence to support the thesis
that in many respects his most radical discontinuity
with Protestant liberalism occurred on this issue. *An
Interpretation of Christian Ethics*, is I think, a Social
Gospel book with respect to the moral normativeness
of the teachings of Jesus; its innovation is primarily in
the interpretation of human agency.[4]

It is not necessary to summarize the widely known
anthropology of *The Nature and Destiny of Man*.
Some observations, however, can be made to show its
distinctive significance. The main line of Christian
theology has always been concerned with the eternal
destiny of persons; the doctrine of man was correlated
with the doctrine of salvation, and salvation pointed to
the saving of persons from their fallenness and finally
the saving of the whole of creation from the effects of
sin. Concerns for moral action and for history were, of
course attended to, but these were usually ancillary
to the soteriological concerns. Reinhold Niebuhr is

little occupied with salvation from sin; he is much occupied with the development of a theological anthropology that accounts for the deceptions and the possibilities of moral and political action in history. And where the significance of salvation is emphasized, such an assurance of mercy and of the coming of the Kingdom of God at the end of history, its import is the effects on the dispositions of historical moral agents; mercy is the ground of a freedom to be prudential and the Kingdom a ground for hope. Both the freedom and the hope are necessary to avoid distortions and pitfalls in political moral activity.[5]

While it is somewhat too simple to argue that the interpretation of human nature in the Gifford Lectures serves only to criticize alternative views in the light of their moral and political consequences, basically such an interpretation is correct. The errors of other views are established by showing the political and moral distortions that result from them. The deepest justification for Niebuhr's Christian view of man (which involves not only man as sinner, but man as self-determining freedom and other elements) is the unmasking of illusions and deceptions, and the unveiling of what humanity 'really' is. It issues in a 'correct analysis' of experience. I illustrate this with an example which comes from Niebuhr's discussions of conscience.

> The significance of the Biblical interpretation of conscience lies precisely in this, that *a universal human experience, the sense of being commanded, placed under obligation and judged* is *interpreted* as a relation between God and man in which it is God who makes demands and judgments upon man. Such an *interpretation* of common experience is not possible without the presuppositions of the Biblical faith. But once accepted the assumption proves to be the only *basis of a correct analysis* of all the factors involved

in the experience; for *it is a fact* that man is judged and yet there is no vantage point in his own life, sufficiently transcendent, from which the judgment can take place.[6]

I take the logic of this and similar passages to be this: there are common (or indeed universal) human experiences. When these experiences are interpreted on the basis of biblical faith they are most accurately understood. The assumptions of biblical faith turn out to be 'the only basis of a correct analysis'. The test of the correct analysis is its efficacy in leading to appropriate kinds of moral and political actions. What is understood on the basis of biblical presuppositions then becomes presuppositional to historical, political, and moral analysis; it is verified in the persuasiveness of its construal of events. As Niebuhr's many secular admirers and allies grasped, one could be persuaded by the 'correct analysis' without being interested in the biblical faith as its only basis.

Both the theological and the philosophical judgements that a theologian makes about human nature affect ethics, or are correlated with ethics. Niebuhr's chapters on the relations of body, mind and spirit function as a biblically backed philosophical anthropology; its stress on the capacity for self-determination can be distinguished from more deterministic accounts of human action. This idea of freedom is not only central to the way in which sin is explained (it creates anxiety which persons overcome through sensuality or pride) but it is also important to ground his view of moral accountability. More deterministic views of human action mitigate that accountability.

More particularly *theological* judgements also affect the ethics. If, for example, one takes the Reformation formula *simul justus et peccator*, the weight that a theologian gives to justification or to sin affects the whole moral outlook. If the weight is on justification, or more heavily on the morally improving consequences of sanctification, there is quite a different tone of ethics from that in which sin is stressed. If grace and its efficacy is emphasized on either purely theological grounds or behavioural grounds the tone of ethics is more joyful and cosmically optimistic than if the emphasis is on sin. Gustaf Wingren's criticism of Barth's theology comes to mind; in the eyes of the Swedish Lutheran (a theological tradition that Barth called strangely Manichean) Barth has no devil and thus his ethics suffer.[7] Niebuhr is on Wingren's side more than on Barth's; there is assurance of mercy and hope, but the grim threats of evil in the world due to the actions of sinners are highlighted. The wisdom of this alerted Niebuhr to the significance of Nazism before American Protestant liberals saw the light; it also predisposed him to support the Cold War and backs contemporary Niebuhrians of the far right in America.[8] Indeed, when one compares the political writings of Niebuhr and Barth in the post-war period one sees the difference between ethics based on the primacy of sin and on the primacy of grace.

4.   The fourth base point of theological ethics is the doctrine of God: what a theologian writes about God and God's relations to the world is correlated with ethical writings. In the Christian tradition, almost all theologians accommodate both transcendence and immanence; which they stress affects ethics. (Or, what the ethician wishes to say affects which he or she stresses.) Niebuhr's polemic against the early Barth is directed against the excessive emphasis on the transcendence of God; in this view all things are relativized equally in Niebuhr's view of the matter, and there is no basis for making discriminating moral and political judgements. The fault of radical immanence is that the 'distance' is overcome between the historically actual

and the transcendent norm or ideal. There is no principle of radical judgement on the historical and the actual. In good dialectical fashion the extreme poles, taken independently of each other, are in error.

Yet I think some generalizations are warranted. Clearly Niebuhr was quite uninterested in exploring process metaphysics as a way to establish the truth of God as having primordial and consequent natures. Just as clearly he did not opt for the conclusions of biblical theologians of his time that the God of the Bible is a God acting in history. The first question of Reinhold Niebuhr's ethics is not the first question of H. Richard Niebuhr's or of Paul Lehmann's, namely 'What is God doing?' While his theology provides symbols and myths for interpreting the meaning of events, both the manner and the outcome of the interpretation, and thus the moral consequences of it, differ from those contemporaries of his. Just as clearly Reinhold Niebuhr does not build his ethics on a Thomistic ontology or the moral order of the creation; indeed, his most prominent arguments against natural law ethics are moral and not theological or philosophical. He was most critical of what he deemed to be the socially conservative consequences of the theory of natural law.

For Niebuhr, I believe that the transcendence of God was finally accented more than the immanence. Like most Protestant views, this provided a basis for grasping the relativities of historical experience and a ground for judgement against all idolatries, all usurping of divine prerogatives. But for Niebuhr it also provided the transcendent norm or ideal which both guided and judged all human actions. Indeed, to make a rather daring generalization, I believe that what Niebuhr says about God are postulates of practical reason, though they rely upon 'revelation' rather than transcendental deductions for their specifications. What he says about God and God's relations to the world establish the conditions of possibility for proper moral and political life: a principle of judgement in the light of which all human activities are seen as finite and sinful; a principle of mercy which enables human agents to be free to act prudentially; and a principle of hope which militates against ultimate meaninglessness and despair.

III. *A* THEOLOGICAL *Profile of Niebuhr's Theological Ethics*

To develop the theological profile would simply be to extract the theological backings of the ethical profile I have drawn, and thus be repetitious. Here it suffices to remind readers that different ethicians select and develop different theological themes, doctrines or symbols so that what they say theologically coheres with what they say ethically. Sufficient comparisons have been provided to establish not only that such choices are made, but also to show the significance of the choices. The theological emphases of Reinhold Niebuhr are demonstrably different from those of, for example, classic Thomistic theologians, Barth, his brother Richard, Paul Lehmann, Moltmann and Panneberg, Karl Rahner, et al. There is coherence between Niebuhr's theological choices and how they are developed on the one hand and his ethics and politics on the other, as is the case in the other theologies I have just named. One critical issue involved is what kind of truth claims are made for theology. Niebuhr's early discussion of the concept of myth is crucial to understanding his theological truth claims. I believe a sentence quoted previously sums up this matter: '[Faith] illumines experience and is in turn validated by experience.' It is experience that validates faith and theology; it is for this reason that I claim that in the end, for Niebuhr, theology was in the service of ethics. They are dialectically related, but in my judgement the weight is on ethics.

NOTES

1. *Beyond Tragedy* pp. 20–21.
2. *The Nature and Destiny of Man* vol. II, p. 63.
3. See Alan Gewirth, *Reason and Morality* (Chicago: University of Chicago Press, 1978), pp. 21–42.
4. *An Interpretation of Christian Ethics.*
5. Dennis McCann is correct to note the importance of a dispositional ethics in Niebuhr that results from his use of Christian doctrines and myths, though McCann is incorrect in the extent to which he reduces Niebuhr's ethics to the dispositional. See Dennis McCann, *Christian Realism and Liberation Theology* (Maryknoll, New York: Orbis Books, 1981), p. 87.
6. *The Nature and Destiny of Man* vol. 1, p. 129 (Italics added).
7. Gustaf Wingren, *Theology in Conflict: Nygren-Barth-Bultmann,* trans. Eric H. Wahlstrom (Philadelphia: Muhlenberg Press, 1958), p. 25.
8. See essays in *Christian Realism and Political Problems.*

Reinhold Niebuhr on Sin: A Critique

DAPHNE HAMPSON

In a fascinating chapter of *The Nature and Destiny of Man* Reinhold Niebuhr analyses sin primarily as pride. In this essay I want firstly to suggest that this analysis is inappropriate for women.[1] Secondly I want to suggest that women's different view of the world and way of inter-relating may help to cure the human situation which Niebuhr depicts. In my analysis I shall draw on the work of Kierkegaard, on whose description of the human Niebuhr bases his own, and I shall make use of recent feminist work on human relations.

I shall not repeat at length Niebuhr's analysis. He follows Kierkegaard closely in his depiction of the human predicament. Kierkegaard, in *The Concept of Dread* and elsewhere, says that man is a double, both tied-to-nature and spirit, having both necessity and possibility. It is this duality, this *Zweispaltung*, which gives rise to anxiety, to *Angst*. Niebuhr, taking this as given, says that in this situation of anxiety man tries to discard his contingent nature and soar to pretensions of absoluteness. The major tradition from Augustine through Luther thus sees sin primarily as pride; sin is that self-centredness whereby the creature in his *hubris* pretends to be adequate of himself, and so sets himself up in the place of God, refusing to be dependent. The ego, says Niebuhr, falsely makes itself the centre of existence in its pride and will-to-power, and in the process inevitably subordinates other life to its will.[2] The devil is patterned upon the nature of man. He is a fallen angel, who fell because he tried to fly higher than God. Niebuhr quotes Isaiah: 'How art thou fallen from heaven, O Lucifer, son of the morning! . . . For thou hast said in thine heart, I will ascend into heaven, I will exalt my throne above the stars of God. Yet thou shalt be brought down to hell.' Commensurately with his understanding of sin, Niebuhr sees love in its highest form as self-sacrificial and involving the breaking of the egotistical desires of the self. Niebuhr also comments, though he hardly analyses this, that another way of reacting to anxiety than in pride is in sensuality; forgetting that he has a spirit, man attempts to bury himself in the natural world.

I am not faulting Niebuhr's analysis. It is surely illuminating. I am simply saying that it is a description of what is a peculiarly male temptation. His analysis reminds me of the discussion of the outlook of boys by Carol Gilligan (a Harvard development psychologist) in her best selling book *In a Different Voice.* Jake, an eleven year old, with great self-confidence and sense of his own importance, sees the world as though he were in the centre of it. Christian theology, written by men, has well understood their problem. Indeed, these myths and stories about pride, and fall, have been formulated because they correspond to a truth. William Temple, whom Niebuhr does not quote, puts it neatly: 'Sin has "I" in the middle.' What I want to say however is that this is inadequate as a description of woman. My criticism is of Niebuhr's equation of male with human.

Kierkegaard's analysis is more subtle and more complex. He keeps a balance between the two kinds of sin, pride and sensuality, and names them as the manly and the womanly forms; though he says that each sex can experience the other form. His view of woman may make her seem somewhat effete, but one has to remember that he is living in the first half of the nineteenth century. Moreover he is describing the sickness typical of each sex, not whole human beings. In a late work, *The Sickness Unto Death* (the 'sickness' being despair, *Angst*), Kierkegaard says that there are two ways of failing to be a self, of being in despair. His concept of the self is that it is a relation, which relates to itself. But the self can only be so related, so integrated, when the spirit which forms the synthesis itself stands in relation to another, to God. There are then two possible ways of being in despair, two ways of failing to be a self. There is the despair of trying to be yourself by yourself, the despair which Niebuhr is to call pride, and which Kierkegaard names as the manly form of despair. And there is the opposite, the despair of not willing to be yourself, of, as Niebuhr would say, losing yourself in sensuality, which Kierkegaard names the womanly.

Such is Kierkegaard's depiction of the two sexes. Woman, he says, 'has [not] the egotistical concept of the self' of the man. She by devotion, which means giving herself away, loses herself. The man by contrast 'has himself'. The woman's despair then consists in weakness: 'her despair is: not to will to be [herself]'. The man by contrast is defiant, despairingly determined to be himself. So the man said of himself that he would either be Caesar or nothing. And since he did not become Caesar, he is in despair. In fact he is in despair over *himself*; since what he wanted, in wishing to become Caesar, was to be rid of himself, the self which he actually is. But the woman attempted to be rid of herself by losing herself in another. The young girl despairs over her lover because he died or was unfaithful. She wanted to lose herself by becoming 'his'. So now she is in despair because she has to be a self without him. That is to say she is in despair over herself, for she does not want to be herself – she wanted to lose herself by becoming 'his'.[3]

Now if this is in any way a description of woman,

then the analysis of sin as pride is for her inappropriate. Both forms of despair are a not willing to be
oneself. But there the similarity ends. The man with
his inflated ego is not content to be himself, but wills
to be another greater than himself. He attempts to
avoid coming to himself; he fails to move inward. For
the woman, by contrast, the failure is a failure to come
to herself, and so she wishes to be rid of herself by
losing herself in another. Far from having an inflated
self, she has hardly begun to find herself. Far from
being an isolated, self-sufficient individual, she has
abnegated responsibility for herself. It is then wide of
the mark to prescribe for her that she should forgo her
pride, or that she should stop exploiting others and
start serving them. Her problem is that she insuffi-
ciently values herself.[4] Her task is to become a differentiated self, a determinate individual, who may say 'I'
without feeling guilty. To tell such a woman that it is
the sin of pride to seek self-fulfilment is to reinforce
her form of sin: her dispersal of herself in others, her
unwarranted serving of them, her attempt to live
through them, and her self-disparagement. Rather
should she dare to love herself, to see that she has a
self – that than which, as Kierkegaard says, next to
God there is nothing as eternal.[5]

Recent feminist work in the field of psychoanalysis
is pertinent here. I am thinking in particular of Jean
Baker Miller's book *Toward a New Psychology of
Women*, again a best seller – and I mention this of her
and Gilligan's books for they have evidently found a
resonance with many women. Miller, a Boston analyst,
in giving case studies of her patients, shows that what
women who are troubled (and not only those who are
troubled) need, is to gain some sense of themselves.
The society, the relations with men and within the
family in which they live, have often dictated against
this. Miller does not attempt to adjudicate between the

influence of societal structures and what may be called
the endemic nature of women; she just reports empirically and observantly on what she sees. But her feminist analysis of the wider social setting within which
therapy takes place is important. Her book is hopeful:
she shows women coming to find new strengths and
self-realization – precisely, coming to themselves.

I have suggested that Niebuhr's discussion of sin as
pride is inappropriate for women. In so far as he discusses sensuality women may well find his description
apposite. Niebuhr writes: 'Sensuality represents an
effort to escape from the freedom and the infinite possibilities of spirit by becoming lost in the detailed
processes, activities and interests of existence, an
effort which results inevitably in unlimited devotion to
limited values.'[6] Valerie Saiving, who in her article
'The Human Situation: A Feminine View' criticizes his
understanding of sin as pride as inadequate as a description of women, portrays women's temptation in
terms which bear a marked resemblance to Niebuhr's
discussion of sensuality. She writes:

> The temptations of woman *as woman* are not the
> same as the temptations of man *as man*, and the
> specifically feminine forms of sin – 'feminine' not
> because they are confined to women or because
> women are incapable of sinning in other ways but
> because they are outgrowths of the basic feminine
> character structure – have a quality which can never
> be encompassed by such terms as 'pride' and 'will-
> to-power'. They are better suggested by such items
> as triviality, distractibility, and diffuseness; lack of
> an organizing center or focus; dependence on
> others for one's own self-definition; . . . – in short
> underdevelopment or negation of the self.

She concludes that: 'the specifically feminine dilemma
is, in fact, precisely the opposite of the masculine.'[7]

Judith Plaskow, who in her book *Sex, Sin and Grace: Women's Experience and the Theologies of Reinhold Niebuhr and Paul Tillich* takes further Saiving's analysis, gives a definition of women's sin which hits the nail on the head. It is, she says, 'the failure to take responsibility for self-actualization'.[8]

I should like to add to this discussion a comment from a Freudian perspective. It is perhaps not without interest that the imagery which theology, which has been male, has thrown up to describe sin is sexually male. Thus pride is described in rising or height metaphors – 'And what is sin', says Augustine, as Niebuhr quotes him, 'but a perverse desire of height?' – often to be followed by a fall which is feared. While sensuality is described in terms of 'losing' oneself in another. Will women find imagery which is appropriate to *their* predicament? Might one not speak of a lack of coming to fruition, of a hollowness, an emptiness, as metaphors for that lack of centredness which is a failure to come to oneself?

To take the analysis one stage further back. For both Kierkegaard and Niebuhr the given is that our nature is dual, and that this duality causes anxiety, out of which sin arises. But do we necessarily sense ourselves as dual and is this a cause of disquiet? Do women find this to be the case? Or are we perhaps concerned here with a peculiarly male dilemma? I doubt that women conceive of themselves in this way. The qustion might be put as follows. Why (from a woman's perspective) are men so curiously unintegrated, so disconnected from mundane reality, so abstracted from the processes of nature? Is it simply centuries of conditioning, of being spared the washing-up and the screaming child? Much theology has indeed been written by men divorced from the daily round of chores, from the human lifecycle of caring and nurturing; theology has been a preoccupation of monks, bishops and professors. No wonder that the human being whom they take as the norm is the isolated male. In his imagination this individual knows no bounds, projecting himself in his possibility, and then becomes anxious because he comes up against nothing. But this is a world away from the attempt to think amid the multifaceted demands of the concretion of everyday existence, to find some space, some 'room of one's own'. It may be that this very entanglement, the need to actualize all sides of oneself at once, leaves women essentially strangers to the flight which men describe. Plaskow writes: 'It could be that women, because they have been associated with nature and natural functions, have necessarily developed a more positive contentful sense of human creatureliness than Niebuhr (men?) and a greater sense of connection with natural processes and needs.'[9] Against which had been written by a previous reader of the library copy of her book which I read: 'Yes, yes, excellent!' Miller comments: 'Women have a much greater sense of the pleasures of close connection with physical, emotional, and mental growth than men.'[10] Perhaps we women are more naturally integrated, more contentedly creatures.

Niebuhr's prescription for doing away with despair is faith. Faith for him is trust, as it is for the Protestant (in particular the Lutheran) tradition on which he draws. Now the faith which is trust is in that tradition, as it is for Niebuhr, precisely an overcoming of egocentricity. As Luther puts it in those lines which form the climax of his 'The Freedom of a Christian' (1520) 'A Christian lives not in himself, but in Christ. . . . Otherwise he is not a Christian. . . . By faith he is caught up beyond himself into God.'[11] For Luther, to be a Christian is to live *extra se*, outside oneself; it is to have a new 'centre of gravity'.[12] The person who is still bound up with himself has not heard the message of the gospel, which is that justification is by faith (trust in another), not by works (self-perfection).[13] Christian living is characterized by a freedom for preoccupation with oneself.

Now Kierkegaard, as I have argued elsewhere,[14] moves away from such an understanding. For his concern is to become a self. Thus he speaks not only of faith, which is trust in another, but of love of God, which involves a dipolar relation with another. It is through a reciprocal relation with God, a relation of love, that he becomes a self. This is very significant. Kierkegaard has to move outside the Lutheran structure to say what he wishes to say. Niebuhr by contrast has no such interest in becoming a self. His interest is in faith, not love. But this is fatal if, as Kierkegaard says, the reason for the man's and the woman's respective sin is a failure to be a 'self'. Thus Niebuhr does not really speak to Kierkegaard's question as to how the man shall cease trying to be Caesar (causing havoc to others in the process) by becoming himself. His answer of 'have faith' precisely does not tolerate the self coming to itself.

Moreover the Lutheran structure to which Niebuhr conforms has at its centre a dichotomy. The self which in sin tries to be adequate of its self must be broken. Niebuhr writes, in an exegesis of St Paul's words in Galatians 2.20, that 'the sinful self, the self which is centred in itself, must be "crucified"; . . . shattered at the very centre of its being'. The Christian experiences a 'new self' which is 'more truly a real self because the vicious circle of self-centredness has been broken'.[15] For this tradition (for Kierkegaard too) it is precisely the failure to come to myself by myself which opens up the possibility of turning to God. Lutheranism is essentially twice-born. Grace does not complete nature. Thus for Bultmann in this tradition I do not take my past into my future as something to be built upon. To be a Christian means to be freed from my past and to live from God's future which is always coming towards me.

But this is bound to seem peculiarly unsatisfactory to women if they as people are essentially interested in biography, in weaving the past into the present, in an introspection conducive to self-transformation. Perhaps it is women's task and women's métier to be interested in growth, in change, in continuity. Why be constantly jumping outside oneself and denying one's past? If women's basic problem is not self-centredness, but rather lack of a sense of self, a scheme of salvation which consists in breaking the self, and in discontinuity with the past, may be unhelpful. The interrelation of love, with God and with others (by contrast with faith) allows one to feel good about oneself. One is affirmed as a self by being loved for oneself, and out of a certain centredness in oneself, loves another.

So to conclude. Gilligan discusses the differing way in which men and women construe relationships by taking the models of 'web'[16] and 'hierarchy'. In the course of her research she has concluded that the women who speak through her tape-recordings have 'a different voice'. Women understand relatedness: they know about the web of human inter-connectedness which makes for life. What they need to learn is that necessary differentiation of the self from others. This fits well with what we have been saying. Men by contrast think in terms of hierarchy and are naturally competitive. They keep others at a distance, fearing close relationships. She writes:

> The images of hierarchy and web, drawn from the texts of men's and women's fantasies and thoughts, convey different ways of structuring relationships and are associated with different views of morality and self. . . . As the top of the hierarchy becomes the edge of the web . . . each image

marks as dangerous the place which the other defines as safe. Thus the images of hierarchy and web inform different modes of assertion and response: the wish to be alone at the top and the consequent fear that others will get too close; the wish to be at the center of connection and the consequent fear of being too far out on the edge.

The task for men is then to learn to find themselves *in relationship*; the task for women, to learn to find *themselves* in relationship. Significantly, women locate the origin of violence in 'the isolation of self and in the hierarchical construction of human relationships'.[17] In one experiment, in which people were given pictures and asked to write stories to go with them, the greatest number of women wrote violent stories to go with a picture which showed a man sitting alone in an office in a high-rise block. Whereas men in a parallel experiment frequently wrote stories which had a violent ending to go with a picture which showed two people sitting peacefully together on a park bench.

Niebuhr may well have been right when he wrote: 'Man's pride and will-to-power disturb the harmony of creation'[18] – and he may have meant 'man' more literally than he knew. We have got to replace the hierarchy with the web. It may be that women have natural gifts here, skills for the future. Perhaps it is the particular genius of women to find ourselves in relation.[19] Women must self-consciously raise to a public level a different way of interacting. Indeed the women's movement has been in large part a manifestation of this. For it may not be too much to say that unless we fast create a participatory rather than a hierarchical society humanity stands scant chance of survival. Niebuhr would not necessarily have disagreed. He was worried by the aspects of male society and public life that feminist women want to transform.

It may however be that Niebuhr's conception of the

human person, which is individualistic rather than social (meaning by 'social' that the person is seen as in relation) does not allow him to conceive of a class, or of a sex, in mutual solidarity with one another changing the order of society. This is coupled with his view that sin is pride and love self-sacrifice, which does not allow him to speak of sin as a failure to assert oneself (or of a group to assert itself) or of love as involving a sense of self worth. Judith Vaughan's evaluation of the ethics of Niebuhr in the light of Rosemary Ruether's work elucidates these points. For Vaughan there are two types of sin, the refusal to relinquish power and the refusal to claim it. Both prevent conditions of alienation, in which the self sees itself as separate from others, or as a mere appendage of others, from being transformed into a situation of community. She writes: 'Niebuhr's perspective inhibits the efforts of women to develop a critical awareness of the essentially oppressive nature of their society, and to respond, angrily and creatively, to change it.'[20] Ruether's ethics by contrast enables those engaged in *claiming* power, as well as those engaged in relinquishing it, to see their activity as moral.[21] We have a responsibility to create something new in history: a society based on inter-relationships.[22]

As a theologian what interests me is that the implications of what I have been saying for our understanding of God are considerable. The God of the tradition, as we have seen, fits the male system. Indeed he seems to have been modelled on the worst image of the human male. He is isolated, powerful, and at the top of the hierarchy. He is said to have aseity: to be entire unto himself! The God of the Old Testament is arbitrary, his writ runs, and he is always right. What kind of a projection is this? Moreover his supremacy qualifies others. It is by comparison with his goodness that men are to know themselves sinners. Thus Niebuhr writes, not untypically for a Christian theologian of this century, that Christianity is: 'a religion of revelation in which a holy and loving God is revealed to man as the source and end of all finite existence against whom the self-will of man is shattered and his pride abased.'[23] Man's ultimate sin is the pride in which he sets himself up in the place of God. Niebuhr comments, echoing Barth, that human religiousness is 'merely a final battleground between God and man's self-esteem'.[24]

May not Freud again shed light here? Have we not a classic case of the absolute taboo that the sons should challenge the father? If God is conceived, as on this model he is, as an Almighty Other, a Father-God, and if it be the case that at some deep level sons both revere and are afraid to challenge fathers, then no wonder this whole dynamic of sin as that pride whereby men try to displace God gets under way. For Niebuhr, as for Protestantism in general, the correct relation to God is one of dependence. That is what it means to be a creature.

If today in many circles, not just feminist circles, words like power, isolation and hierarchy have negative not positive connotations, then we shall scarcely want to conceive of God in these terms. If our ideal model for human society is the web and not the hierarchy, then God as God has previously been conceived will be left stranded high and dry – at best irrelevant. God will need to be seen as involved in the web, supporting it, spinning it. God is the one who moves among us, providing the context of our lives. Perhaps indeed God ceases to be a separate entity. If men have conceived of God after their individual image, should not women reconceive God after their collective image?

Far from undermining our self-integrity and 'shattering' our selves, God becomes the one who allows us to come into being. God enables us to fulfil the potential of what we have it in us to be. Women in the women's movement speak of 'hearing one another into being'. God becomes supremely that which hears us into being. Attributes of God will need to be reconceived. Thus power becomes not something which is exercised, but the empowering of people. God no longer competes with us, a separate entity, superior to all others, but is that which is creative of our relatedness. God does not stand in contradiction to, but is commensurate with, our vision of human relationships and society.

How far the inherited picture of God is alien to women today was brought home to me by the following incident. While writing this essay I mentioned to a friend of mine, telling her nothing of the essay's content, that in the tradition the devil was said to be an angel who fell because he tried to fly higher than God. Her spontaneous response: 'What sort of a God is that that "He" should mind that an angel should try to fly higher than "Him"?!' A different evaluation of society, of the individual and of human relations cannot but significantly affect our understanding of God.

Miller writes:

> Until recently, 'mankind's' understandings have been the only understandings generally available to us. As other perceptions arise – precisely those perceptions that men, because of their dominant position could NOT perceive – the total vision of human possibilities enlarges and is transformed. The old is severely challenged.[25]

NOTES

1. For previous work on this theme cf. Valerie Saiving Goldstein, 'The Human Situation: A Feminine View', *Journal of Religion* 40 (Apr. 1960), pp. 100–112, reprinted in ed. C.P. Christ and J. Plaskow, *Womanspirit Rising: A Feminist Reader in Religion* (Harper and Row, 1979); Judith Plaskow, *Sex, Sin and Grace: Women's Experience and the Theologies of Reinhold Niebuhr and Paul Tillich* (University Press of America, 1980); Judith Vaughan, *Sociality, Ethics and Social Change: A Critical Appraisal of Reinhold Niebuhr's Ethics in the Light of Rosemary Radford Ruether's Works* (University Press of America, 1983).

2. *The Nature and Destiny of Man*, vol. I, p. 179.

3. *The Sickness Unto Death*, ed. and trans. H.V. and E.H. Hong (Princeton University Press, 1980) pp. 49–50.

4. It may be that men seek to overcome anxiety typically by outward aggression, whereas women turn in on themselves. Those maladies which tend to be women's maladies may be said to be self-destructive, or the result of an inadequate sense of self: anorexia, claustrophobia and agoraphobia. Men fight in pubs, women swallow sleeping pills and silently destroy themselves.

5. Kierkegaard *op.cit.*, p. 53.

6. Niebuhr *op.cit.*, p. 185.

7. Saiving *op.cit., Womanspirit Rising*, pp. 37, 39.

8. *Op.cit.*, p. 3.

9. *Ibid*, p. 71.

10. (Beacon Press, 1976), p. 40.

11. Ed. J. Dillenberger, *Martin Luther: Selections from His Writings* (Anchor Books, 1961), p. 80.

12. The phrase owes to Philip Watson. *Let God be God: An Interpretation of the Theology of Martin Luther* (Epworth Press, 1947), p. 34.

13. Emma Trout writes of the doctrine of justification by faith that whereas it was 'a beautifully freeing experience' for Luther and is helpful to men, who tend to think both that they can and ought to go it alone and accomplish things, it is subversive of women who are 'taught to be non-aggressive, to fail, to set limited goals'. Women need to be encouraged to think that they should take on the responsibility of acting in the world and come into their own. 'The Doctrine of Justification in the Light of Sexual Differences.' (Unpublished paper, 1970), pp. 17–18.

14. 'The Self's Relation to God: A Study in Faith and Love.' (Unpublished Harvard Th.D. thesis, 1983, ch. IV.)

15. *The Nature and Destiny of Man*, vol. II, pp. 108–110.

16. The word web has come to have particular connotations in feminist discourse. It connotes not only that relations are on a horizontal plane as opposed to a vertical-hierarchical plane, but the resultant weaving together of those things which make for life, in the face of that which is destructive. Women in the peace movement, and in women's liturgies, have symbolized this using wool. See also Mary Daly's depiction of women as 'spinners'. She writes: 'Gyn/Ecological creativity is spin-

ning ... - discovering the lost thread of connectedness within the cosmos, repairing this web as we create.' *Gyn/Ecology: The Metaethics of Radical Feminism* (The Women's Press, 1979), p. 390.

17. (Harvard University Press, 1982), pp. 62, 45.

18. *The Nature and Destiny of Man*, vol. I, p. 179.

19. Cf. Miller *ibid*, pp. 42–43: 'While men do enter into some forms of concerted endeavor, the prevailing values in the settings in which most men spend their lives make it extremely difficult to sustain it. Moreover, in the family setting, men very early in life acquire the sense that they are members of a superior group. Things are supposed to be done for them by those lesser people who work at trying to do so. From then on, cooperativeness may appear to men as if it were somehow detracting from themselves. To cooperate, to share, means somehow to lose something, or at best, altruistically, to give something away. All this is greatly augmented by men's notions that they must be independent, go it alone, win.

To women, who do not have the same experience, cooperativeness does not have the same quality of loss.'

20. *Op.cit.*, p. 195.

21. For a similar analysis from a (non-feminist) Marxist perspective see John C. Raines, 'Sin as Pride and Sin as Sloth', *Christianity and Crisis* (Feb. 3, 1969), pp. 4–8. Raines writes (p. 5): '[Niebuhr's] keen insight into the self-love, pride and pretentiousness of man needs to be balanced with Marx's sensitivity to the self-loss, passivity and false consciousness that seduce and vitiate mankind from the opposite direction.'

22. It is interesting that it is a women, Karen Horney, whom Niebuhr criticizes for thinking that the will-to-power springs from the general insecurities of a competitive civilization and therefore holding out hope for its elimination in a co-operative society. *The Nature and Destiny of Man*, vol. I, p. 192.

23. *Ibid*, p. 201.

24. *Ibid*, p. 200.

25. *Op.cit.*, p. 1.

Reinhold Niebuhr and the Christian Hope

KEITH WARD

One of the characteristic features of the semitic religions – Judaism, Christianity and Islam – is their emphasis on the importance of history and of the pursuit of social morality. Some other religious traditions regard history as ultimately of little importance, as a realm of illusion or sport, without a clear goal or purpose. The aim of the religious life is then often seen as a seeking to escape from the round of ills and suffering which is *samsara*. Such release is for the individual soul, and only the individual can accomplish it, by long and arduous ascetic discipline. The semitic traditions have quite a different emphasis. In the Hebrew Bible, the world is seen as created by God for a good purpose. The aim of the religious life is to worship God, but to do so by building a society of justice and peace on earth, by living in the world in accordance with the will of God. The Christian tradition takes this emphasis even further by its central claim that God became incarnate in the flesh, thereby sanctifying the material world and making it a positive sacrament of the Divine presence. And, in its testimony to the resurrection of Jesus from death, it presents a clear hope for the coming of the Kingdom of God as the goal of human life and of creation itself.

Thus the Christian faith enshrines as a central part of its teaching a positive hope for the material world and a positive purpose for the historical process. The world of history is not simply to be escaped from. It is somehow to be transfigured, renewed, redeemed, to express fully the purpose of a loving God. In this sense, Christianity is and always must be a worldly and materialist faith. Insofar as its hope is for a society of justice and peace, wherein God's will can be clearly expressed, its hope is political – it is about the founding and sustenance of a *polis*, a city or society of persons, bound together in the love of God.

But how, exactly, is this hope to be conceived? And what implications, if any, does it have for the political ideals and principles of Christians in this confused and violent world? Among those who have wrestled with this problem in the course of Christian history, Reinhold Niebuhr is a central figure. He was always primarily concerned to relate the Christian gospel to the realities of the political world. And, in the course of a long and active life of involvement in social action in the United States of America, he developed a sensitive and realistic conception of the way in which the Christian hope relates to present political issues and concerns. My aim in this paper is to look at some of the things Niebuhr said about the Christian understanding of eschatology and its implications for political thought. Of course, any such account needs to be prefaced by acknowledgement that Niebuhr's thought moved through many stages, and that it cannot be considered as one non-developing system. Nevertheless, certain central concerns and ways of approach are present throughout his thought; and I will seek to use those concerns in helping to develop what may be called a Niebuhrian view of these matters – for I would not claim to give a definitive statement of his own views. Rather, my concern is to develop an approach to the question of Christian political hope which is faithful to the methods and insights of Niebuhr's work, without seeking to give either a historical account of his work or a systematic presentation of his ideas.

In the Preface to the 1956 edition of *An Interpretation of Christian Ethics*, Niebuhr writes, 'The primary issue is how it is possible to derive a social ethic from the absolute ethic of the gospels'.[1] This issue is a major problem in Niebuhr's view, because of two contrasting factors – on the one hand, the absolute, perfectionist and rigorist teaching of the 'Sermon on the Mount'; and, on the other hand, the fact of ineradicable human self-interest, which makes it necessary to see social life as a permanent and unavoidable conflict or, at best, balancing of interests. Thus he spoke often of Christian moral commands as 'impossible possibilities', a paradoxical expression which served to negate both naturalism (which he characterizes as the view that Christ's commands of love are unrealistic and so should be dropped) and Utopianism (the view that the Kingdom of God is a historical possibility, whether by human progress or catastrophic Divine intervention).

That the primary issue for Christian ethics can only be satisfactorily stated in a paradox is often stressed by Niebuhr, and he spells out something of the thinking behind it in an evocative essay, 'As Deceivers, Yet True', in 1938.[2] Religious symbols, he there holds, are supra-rational. They state facts which are beyond any possibility of consistent rational systematization. He held that it was not possible to frame a final, consistent, rationally coherent metaphysical picture of the world. No doubt he felt, like Kant, that the paths of metaphysics were so strewn with wreckage that further attempts were foredoomed to failure. But he did not, like Kant, make the further attempt to end all further attempts. Rather, he wished to hold together various symbols of the human condition in tension, as giving supra-rational insight into the 'eternal as revealed and expressed in that temporal'. Consequently, each religious symbol is in one sense false or deceiving. The

New Testament vision of the apocalypse, which he thought was probably shared by Jesus in at least some respects *could* be taken as a historical illusion. In *The Nature and Destiny of Man*, he writes that 'The belief of an age that it has reached the end of history is pathetic'.[3] To hold such a belief is to believe something false. Yet, taken 'seriously but not literally', that symbol of the Parousia and the Kingdom of God expresses a truth. It is 'a mythical expression of the impossible possibility under which all human life stands'.[4] That is, there will not be an establishing of the Kingdom in history. Niebuhr is quite adamant on that point. In *The Nature and Destiny of Man*, he writes, 'Where there is history at all there is freedom; and where there is freedom there is sin'.[5] The only reality where conflicts are overcome is eternity. This eternity is neither a continuation of history and time, nor a timeless, static blankness in which history has no significance. 'The eternal can only be fulfilled in the temporal'[6]; yet in the eternal, 'the contradictions of human existence . . . are swallowed up in the life of God himself'.[7]

'Faith in God', he writes, 'means faith in the transcendent unity of essence and existence'.[8] There is a consummation; a resolution of conflicts; but it transcends the limits of the conceivable; it is not a human possibility. All we can say is that 'eternal significance belongs to each moment of our existence, and to historical existence taken as a whole'.[9] The point of paradox is to gesture towards this eternal consummation of the temporal; to use symbols to express the inconceivable; and to deny one-sided and literalist interpretations of those symbols, which turn religious assertions into pseudo-historical or scientific predictions.

This is, or at least it implies, a rich and complex doctrine of the nature of religious language, and of

the role of paradox in Christian ethics. A main emphasis of this doctrine is the idea that religious truth lies
beyond reason, or somehow states the inconceivable.
It is undoubtedly the case that major elements of
Christian tradition embody this doctrine. The doctrines
of Incarnation and the Trinity have often been said to
be mysteries beyond the power of unaided human
reason to devise or comprehend. And the notion of
God's ineffability is well embedded in the teachings of
the early Fathers. So it may only be possible to speak
in paradox of what is beyond the rational. Paradox is
not just contradiction, however. Contradiction is the
assertion and the denial of the same property to the
same thing at the same time and in the same respect;
it simply succeeds in conveying no information at all.
Whereas paradox states two apparently opposed propositions, both of which are incomplete or inexact in
some way, and each of which is said to be necessary
to a fuller, but still imperfect, understanding of a
peculiarly elusive object. For a paradox to be sustain-
able, there must be appropriate reason why understanding should be imperfect in the area in question; and
why the opposed propositions give greater understanding than either alone, or some alternative, more
comprehensive expression.

In the case of God, there is good reason why
human understanding should be imperfect. It is part of
the theistic hypothesis that the Divine nature is so
superior to human nature, or to any finite nature, that
conceptual frameworks which are devised primarily to
categorize and systematize parts of finite reality might
be expected to falter when applied to such a different,
and indeed unique category of object (by 'object' I
mean object of reference, of course, and not finite,
limited substance, which God is not).

But how do we know which propositions can give
greater understanding of God? Where do we derive

them from? And how do we know how to interpret them? Niebuhr has, in one sense, and perhaps to his own surprise, a very high view of biblical revelation. He does not simply discard the reported teachings of Jesus where they are inconvenient, or deny awkward doctrines, developed from biblical interpretation, of Original Sin and the Second Coming of Christ. On the contrary, he accepts them as providing insights unperceived by reasoning alone. Even though his overt appeal is to the nature of human experience and its analysis, he in practice accepts a set of concepts derived from biblical tradition to analyse experience, and does not drop them when they seem difficult at first. He gives to these biblical concepts, however, a powerful and original interpretation, taking religious symbols to be expressions of the relation of the historical to the eternal, applicable to every historical moment in the life of man.[10] It is clear that reason still serves a vital double role in religion. It must evaluate the claims of competing revelations as to their probable truth; and it must seek to provide a coherent interpretation of the 'revealed' tradition, ordering its very diverse materials in accordance with some criteria of rational acceptability. Thus, while the orthodox Christian doctrine of the Trinity might not be established by rational reflection alone, it must first be rationally decided that the biblical revelation of the Divine nature is probably true. Then particular models of the Trinitarian nature of God must be presented as the most coherent and reasonable interpretations of the biblical material, in the light of other known scientific and philosophical considerations. That the final doctrine may contain paradoxes which reason cannot resolve is no objection to it, as long as there are good reasons for accepting the revelation and for interpreting it in the suggested way. Indeed, it is a further vindication of the internal claim of the religious system to be revelatory of a being so perfect as to be beyond full human comprehension.

The doctrines of the supra-rationality of religious symbols, and of the acceptance of biblical revelation in what must be a non-literal way (since the literal applies only to the finite, and not to God) are important doctrines. They need to be continually re-stressed, in opposition to the encroachments of an over-systematizing rationalism or of a literalistic fundamentalism which reduces God to some sort of very great but finite superperson.

That being said, however, there remains a centrally important question for the interpretation of biblical symbols. To what extent is it part of the internal logic of biblical revelation that it refers to specific historical events or to the actual course of history? Accepting that the primary underlying reference of all religious assertions must be to God, and thus to the eternal, is it nevertheless essential to a biblical understanding of the eternal that it is expressed in specific historical events and that it directs the world towards a proper historical goal?

Niebuhr, in addressing this question, is perfectly clear in his rejection of what he terms 'mysticism' – the view that the historical process has no ultimate purpose, value or meaning, and that only by the absorption of the individual into the Eternal can the religious goal be achieved. He does wish to give history its own purpose and value. In fact, he speaks of the expectation of Christ as 'the expectation of the disclosure and fulfilment of the meaning of history at a point in history, or at the end of history.'[11] History, he says, is 'an interim' between the disclosure of meaning in the cross of Christ and its fulfilment.[12] It is 'still waiting for its culmination in the second coming'.[13] It 'moves towards the realization of the Kingdom'.[14] In these and many similar passages, it sounds as if he wishes to give particular occurrences in history a decisive significance; as if Christ does disclose in a special way the meaning of history; as if history progresses towards a goal; as if that goal will be achieved at some point in history.

And yet he explicitly denies all these expectations. Of the Fall he says that it does not represent an event in history, but is a symbol applicable to every historical moment in the life of man. Of Jesus he says, 'the Jesus of history . . . created the Christ of faith in the life of the early church'.[15] This was mythologized as a sinless life; but he does not think it is possible for there to be an actually sinless life in history, whether of Jesus or of anyone else. The ideal stands above every actuality; and 'interpretations which define the sinlessness . . . of Christ in . . . metaphysical terms can have no real illumination for human conduct'.[16] Jesus is not a miraculous Divine intervention into human history, the sinless redeemer who shows the historical possibility of a perfect human life. On the contrary, a miraculously caused perfection could have no relevance for us normal mortals. So it is 'vicarious suffering' which is 'the final revelation of meaning in history'.[17] And goodness can only exist, even partially, by the renunciation of power. There is no historical possibility of freedom from sin: 'the Kingdom of God is an impossibility in history';[18] and Christian hope must be 'in the fulfilment of life beyond the limitations of temporal existence'.[19]

The picture that Niebuhr finally presents could therefore be taken at first sight as one of profound historical pessimism. His contempt for Liberalism and its utopian dreams is often expressed. There may be growth of some sort in history; but there is no progress apparent, in a moral or spiritual sense. Technology may change; but morality remains as primitive as ever.[20] The dominant model of God becomes that of

the sufferer, who is involved in and suffers with history; who discloses to us an ideal of the renunciation
of power which we cannot wholly embrace without
also renouncing our social responsibilities, who offers
us a fulfilment of meaning and purpose, but in a trans-
historical and indeed inconceivable eternity. In an
essay on 'The Fulfilment of Life', Niebuhr writes, 'To
believe that the body is resurrected is to say . . . that
history is fulfilled in eternity'.[21] What sort of fulfilment
of history is it that can only be effected in eternity? To
explore this question, we need to return to the New
Testament documents; and I think it is possible to see
there how Niebuhr comes to take the view he does.

There is little doubt that the first generation Christians
expected an imminent Judgement Day (Cf. 1 Thess.
4.16–17; 2 Thess. 2.1–10; 1 Pet. 4.7; 2 Pet. 3.3–13; 1
Cor. 15.51–2). The writers of some of the earliest Christian documents have believed that, within their lifetimes, the world would perish in fire. They believed
that they and the dead would meet Christ 'in the air',
and that the wicked would be destroyed. They looked
for the return of the Lord, coming 'like a thief in the
night'; and they prayed for the 'new age' to dawn soon,
when the dead would rise to judgement, evil would be
eradicated from creation and the just and faithful would
enter eternal life. So they thought that the present
world-order would end, within their generation; that
the Day of the Lord, the day of terrible judgement
would come; and that the Spirit of God would then be
poured out on all people. A new, incorruptible world-
order would begin, under the Davidic Kingship of
Christ, the glorified Son of Man.

Within the context of these beliefs, there is no
doubt that Jesus promised his disciples that they
would be members of this renewed Kingdom, for
which the prophets had longed. They would possess
eternal life – life in relation to the Eternal. They would

rise in a new order, to a world of joy and personal fulfilment. There is here a clear promise for the future, couched in the poetic terms of Jewish Apocalyptic. The promise is that there will be a life with God, which will be a fulfilment and not just a denial of this present life. Those who learn to rely solely on God and to do his will, are to find that God will renew and fulfil their lives.

We know that the world did not end in fire in that generation; and this fact has always presented Christian theology with a fundamental task of re-interpretation. One response has been to continue believing in a sudden, cataclysmic ending to world history, but to keep deferring it, until the Gospel has been preached to the whole world, perhaps. But this response is forced to ignore the continual emphasis of the New Testament that all this would happen 'in this generation', and that it would be seen by some of the first disciples before they died. Another response is to stress the highly symbolic character of these promises, and say that the Kingdom is to be realized progressively in history, by human action in co-operation with the action of God. But nothing can be said, on this view, of the resurrection of the dead or their sharing in the new age of the Kingdom. A third response is to make the Kingdom purely a matter of personal life after death, rather than that of a new creation. But that seems to ignore all that is said about the return of Christ in glory, the culmination of world-history in the attainment of a community of the just. Needless to say, there are other interpretations, too, many of which evacuate the doctrine of the Kingdom of any future reference at all, and speak of it as fulfilled in Jesus' resurrection or the outpouring of the Spirit at Pentecost. But that seems to deprive the fervent prayer of the earliest Christians – 'Come, Lord Jesus' – of real significance. Christians have always looked for an appearing of Christ in glory, and a fulfilment of his promises in future.

These are all revisions of the early doctrine, as we have it set out in the New Testament. One thing is certain – that we cannot now believe just what many of the first disciples evidently believed – namely, that they would see the end of the age and the return of Christ in judgement within their lifetimes. As Niebuhr says, that would be for us a pathetic illusion. The subsequent theological history of Christian hope must be based on the need to re-interpret that belief.

In fact the Gospels already contain the resources for dealing with that problem of re-interpretation. Jesus says, 'If by God's finger I expel demons, then the Kingdom came upon you' (Luke 11.20). It is already present, it has drawn near, in the teaching and actions of Jesus himself. When he was asked where the Kingdom would come, he said, 'The Kingdom does not come with seeing . . . it is within (or among – *entos*) you' (Luke 17.20). It starts to become real in the hearts of men and women, as they hear the words of Jesus and turn to follow him. 'The time has been fulfilled and the Kingdom of God has drawn near', he proclaims (Mark 1.15). As he speaks to men and women, it is very near them, even among them. 'The law and prophets existed until John; from then the Kingdom is proclaimed, and all press into it' (Luke 16.16). So the people are already entering the Kingdom, as they hear the words of Jesus and obey. 'Unless a man is born from above, he cannot see the Kingdom' (John 3.3). It is a present spiritual reality, which can be seen and entered only by those 'who do the will of my Father' (Matt. 7.21). Perhaps the best way of putting the emphasis that exists in the proclamation by Jesus of the Kingdom is in the words of John's gospel: 'The time is coming and now is . . . when the Father is worshipped in spirit and in truth' (John. 4.23).

So it is that the disciples are, even now, in the Kingdom; but its fulness, when all tears shall be wiped
away and peace and justice shall reign, is yet to come.
The Kingdom is both a present inward and spiritual
reality; and a symbol for the ultimate fulness of God's
rule and victory over evil. Jesus was, according to the
Gospel records, a man whose life blazed with a sense
of the presence and reality of God, of his judgement
on the evil of the world and on the overwhelming joy
of his promises of fulfilment. He stood within the prophetic tradition of Israel, using the cosmic and mythical imagery of Daniel, Ezekiel and the poets who
invented the fantastic imagery of the Apocryphal writings, to speak of the political and spiritual situation of
the people of their day. He saw Israel at a moment of
crisis in its history. He foresaw the destruction of Jerusalem and the ending of the old dispensation to
Israel, symbolized by the Temple and the sacrifices.
But what he preached was not the gloom and doom of
Jeremiah; instead, he preached the good news of the
Day of Jubilee, the outpouring of the Spirit, the dawning of the Kingdom and the rule of God. Not only did
he preach it; by all accounts, he began to make it
happen in his own person; healing, exorcizing, forgiving and baptizing his followers with the Holy Spirit
(Mark 1.8). As the people followed him, they were
already pressing into the Kingdom, a new way of life,
suffused by the Spirit of God, lived by total loyalty to
him.

So part, and perhaps the most important part, of
Jesus' teaching about the Kingdom is that it is both a
completion and a negation of the expectations of the
Old Testament prophets. Ezekiel had looked for a restoration of the Davidic monarchy in Jerusalem, a
return of all Jewish exiles to the Holy Land and the
establishment of Israel as a leading world-power. Jesus
transforms all these expectations. He is himself the

awaited King, the son of David who will possess the throne of Israel for ever. But he is not the ruler of a political Kingdom – 'My Kingdom is not of this world' (John 18.36). He rules at the right hand of God – that is, with Divine authority and power. But it is a spiritual and inward power; and it is more than external rule. Christ lives in the hearts of those who follow him; they are bound together in him, as members of one body. There is an inward and spiritual union between the disciple and his Lord, so that the King is within, and the subject is ruled, not by external command, but by the Spirit working within to elicit and encourage his own proper gifts and capabilities. That is why we enter the Kingdom when we hear the words of the King, and gladly submit to his rule. The apostles saw the Kingdom already, as they walked in the presence of the King. But after his resurrection and ascension, this Kingship took on a new and more interior form, as the Eternal Word of God began to rule in the lives of men and women in a dramatically new way.

Moreover, the establishment of the Kingdom is not the physical return of exiles to Jerusalem. For Jesus quite clearly teaches that the Kingdom will be taken from those who had the care of it, and thrown open to the whole world (Matt. 21.43). It will no longer be a national state of Israel, for one ethnic group; but a universal faith, open to all, whatever their race or culture. It is not the Jewish exiles who will be gathered home but people of all nations who will be gathered to the presence of the King and the heavenly city, Jerusalem above, the city of God. There will be a 'new Israel'; and this is a radical transformation of Jewish prophetic expectation.

This new Israel will not become a leading world-power, for it is not to be a geographical or political State. It is to be the servant of all. Just as the Son of Man did not come to be served (Mark 10.45), so the people of his Kingdom must be his body in the world, serving, healing and forgiving others. So it can be seen that Jesus' proclamation of the Kingdom, though it built on the tradition of the prophets and used their imagery and symbolism, was yet quite radically new. It transformed the whole idea of the Kingdom into that of an inward and universal community of hearts, united by the out-pouring of the Holy Spirit under the Kingship of the one anointed by God to show his will and purpose for this world.

The imagery of the Apocalypse, so strange and unfamiliar to us, finds its interpretation in this transformation of the prophetic idea of the Davidic Kingdom. Isaiah used cosmic imagery of the stars falling, the sun and moon being darkened and the earth being shaken to its core, to comment on the political conditions of his day. He was representing the defeat of Judah, the exile and the restoration in cosmic terms; but his real theme was the destruction of Babylon and the return to Jerusalem. Many of the prophets speak of a terrible 'Day of the Lord', when judgement will be brought upon the oppressing nations of the world. And they look for a time of renewal, when the Spirit will restore those who are penitent and faithful, and when God's promises to his people will be fulfilled at last.

Jesus takes up these themes and uses this imagery in his teaching. So he speaks of the destruction of Jerusalem and the end of the age of the Temple sacrifices. He speaks of political disaster for Israel, but also of the offer of new life for those who are penitent and who follow him. When he speaks of the coming of the Son of Man in clouds of glory, bringing with him the faithful remnant, the reference is at least partly to the symbolism of the Book of Daniel, to the defeat of worldly powers by a truly human community, which takes people out of the world into the city of God, ruled by the Spirit. Speaking at a time of great political crisis in Israel, when there were many political Messiahs, many uprisings against the tyranny of Rome, and when the whole country was in fact about to be destroyed, he naturally cast his message of the new thing that God was doing through him, in the thought-forms of apocalypse, judgement and the dawning of a new age.

Thus there are two important elements of Jesus' teaching about the Kingdom. First, it is an ethical and spiritual reality in the present, which you enter by following Christ. Second, it is a new thing that God does in history, destroying the Temple and its sacrifices in judgement, creating a new Israel which is to gather people from the ends of the earth, proclaiming the good news of God's saving and fulfilling love. But there is a third element, too. Jesus undoubtedly teaches that there will be a judgement, when we will reap what we have sown, whether for life or for destruction (Matt. 13.30; 13.49). There will be a resurrection to a form of life incorruptible and strong, a life with God and with all those who love him. There will be a final eradication of evil, a re-making of the earth and a sharing in the vision of God by the living and the dead. And there will be a 'parousia', a making-present of Christ in glory, when he finally rules, unopposed, as King of creation. Here again, Jesus used the imagery of the Apocalyptic tradition; and he used it in a way which led his disciples to expect his return in judgement and glory very soon. They had seen him perform miracles and heard him teach of the new relationship to God he offered. They had seen him after his death. They had experienced the amazing gift of the Holy Spirit, poured out upon them at Pentecost. They had been commissioned to proclaim his teaching throughout the whole world. Now they waited for him to return, with eager expectation (Cf. Acts 2.14–36). They believed that they were living in the 'last days', and that the people must escape from the coming judgement by repenting and receiving the gift of the Spirit.

At the same time, what they expected was a 'new creation' not just some sort of social revolution. When Jesus spoke of the resurrection of the dead, he asserted that 'they neither marry nor are given in marriage, but are like angels in heaven' (Matt. 22.30). In the new age, both living and dead will live together, in a world in which there is no longer sun or sea (Rev. 21.1 and 21.23). These are highly symbolic utterances, but they point to a fulfilment in a world radically unlike the present earth. They do not seem to envisage a gradual transformation of the earth into some future just society; but rather some quite different form of existence (one recalls Paul's assertion that 'flesh and blood cannot inherit the Kingdom' in 1 Cor. 15.50), in which the possibilities of this present age can be fulfilled.

Niebuhr seems to be quite right, then, in asserting that the Kingdom of God is not something that could be progressively realized in history by human action. He is also right in saying that, though all earthly history will be broken by sin, yet human history is not just pointless or purposeless. It has a purpose and it does realize important values that would not otherwise exist. But the completion of that purpose lies beyond history, in a realm wherein its values are fully realized in a different form of existence that grows out of this one, while radically transforming it – even as the resurrected Christ really was Jesus, who was raised from death; but he was raised in a different form, glorious and incorruptible, at once vindicating and completing his earthly life.

The Apocalyptic symbols portray the relation between finite creatures and the infinite Creator in terms of analogies drawn from the finite world. As the creation story (or stories) in Genesis speak in terms of temporal days of creation, but are not to be taken literally, so the stories of the end of time, of an imminent appearing of Christ, a resurrection and Day of Judgement, express the relation of finite things to the will of God. The creation is not a matter of temporal beginning, even though God's purposes are worked out in time. And the end of the age is not a matter of a temporal end-point, even though the purposes of God must be worked out in time. What is happening is that a vast temporal process is being depicted from the point of view of its final end and fulfilment, portrayed as a particular event in the near future. Christ shows the goal of the creation of humanity; we shall share in the realization of that goal; and evil will not triumph, but will be transfigured by good. Those are the spiritual realities underlying the mythological forms of Apocalyptic.

People of Jesus' day had no idea at all of the vastness of the cosmos; of the process of evolution; of the rule of physical law and the span of human history. Their world was small; their history was short. About 63 generations ago, Adam had been created; and in one or two generations' time God's purpose would be fulfilled, with a Day of Judgement and Resurrection, in which Christ would play a key role. Once our horizons expand, we must fit Jesus into a long human history, which is itself a peripheral set of events at the age of a small galaxy. The whole complex of images must undergo a dimensional shift. We have to say that we are talking about the relation of each moment of history to its fulfilment in the eternal, trans-historical life of God. Just as it would be a mistake to think of creation as something that happened a long time ago (since we depend on God now and at every time); so it is a mistake to think of the goal of creation as something that lies far in the future of the cosmos (for we find fulfilment in relation to God now and at every time). Of course there was a beginning of human life on earth; and there will presumably be an end of human life on earth. But the creation is not just the beginning, the 'first push' which leaves everything else untouched. It is the continual sustaining of the world by the Divine presence and power. Similarly, the fulfilment is not just the last moment, leaving everything that goes before it as unfulfilled, a mere means to some end beyond. It is the continual transfiguration of every present by its relation to the Eternal, beyond the linear process of time, giving to each moment a proper fulfilment and completion in relation to the trans-temporal goal.

As the great saints and mystics of the Christian tradition have always seen, eternal life is not just some future continuation of this life for ever. It is life in relation to the eternal God. That eternal God cannot be rationally, systematically and clearly conceived by us; for all our concepts are limited to finite and temporal applications. The Unlimited is expressed in and through the historical process. It can even be spoken of as being unfolded in time, as finding new creative self-expression in the temporal process. But it is never bounded by time; and, while it may be spoken of as acting, responding and creating at particular moments of time; it also stands beyond time, both as its origin and basis and as its goal and fulfilment. Such a God can only be spoken of in paradox; he can only be expressed in imaginative symbols, which always need to be qualified by complementary symbols. So God is beyond the furthest galaxies, yet nearer to us than breathing. He is at the end of time, yet in each moment completely. He is unknowable and unlimited, yet the Father of all, responding lovingly to the prayers of his children. Affirmation and negation must always go together when speaking of God, in a double move-

ment of the mind, which at once affirms the highest
we can conceive and also denies, saying continually,
'not that; not that'.

So the end, the final purpose and goal, the meaning
and fulfilment of all things is in God. Standing as we
do as small parts of the vast process of cosmic time,
we may see this fulfilment as infinitely far away. And
yet our own lives do not only contribute to it as dis-
posable means. They are in a strange way parts of it;
and when they are seen as parts, within the totality of
meaning which is the whole of creation, they share in
the End immediately. Is the fulfilment of God's purpose future or altogether beyond time? Paradoxically,
we have to say: both. It is not now; for we are incomplete, sinful, estranged and far from our true selves.
Yet is is not just at some future point in linear time, as
though most of history was destined never to share in
it. The End is 'now and not yet', always imminent and
always unrealized, future and timeless. The End is
beyond time; but precisely as such, it is present in
every time as the eternal fulfilment of each moment;
and each moment is transfigured by its relation to the
whole which it helps to constitute.

So it is that we can watch for the end of all things,
breaking into the present, both negating and fulfilling
the present moment by its inclusion in the eternal. Of
course, particular purposes are set and achieved, to a
greater or lesser extent, in history. Not every time
stands in precisely the same relation to eternity. We
each have appropriate goals to aim at, demands to
respond to, obstacles to overcome. The historical process itself moves to emergent goals, to new levels of
activity and experience, progressively achieved. But
beyond all these things stands the immutable origin
and end of all things, the one who is both Alpha and
Omega, whose end is in his beginning. We stand
within the historical process with our own partial

goals and our own failures to achieve them fully. And we stand in relation to the infinite and eternal God, in whom all things have their origin and find their true completion. So we must look both to the future, to where our lives will find their aims realized; and to the eternal, where all process is already complete in the self-realizing totality of God.

When Jesus proclaims the Kingdom of God, he speaks, in the imagery of the poets of Israel, of the end of all things, the consummation of God's purposes for his human creation. This is to be found in the parousia, the full manifestation of Christ in glory, the inner union of God and human nature which is established in Christ and fulfilled in us by our union with him. It will bring a decisive crisis of judgement for each life, in which what we have made ourselves will be made clear and open; in which we shall each finally find that we have placed ourselves in the outer darkness of self, or that we will be able to accept the freely offered love of God to renew and remake us in an incorruptible and eternal life. We cannot defer this moment of decisive choice to some far future. We make it now, as we respond to God's initiative of love. So we must always watch and keep alert, as if at each moment the final apotheosis was at hand.

We are to watch for the final goal of all things, breaking into each present, determining our eternal relationship to God. This is the spiritual reality behind the imagery of an imminent Day of Judgement and Return of the Son of Man with his chosen ones to reign in glory – there is to be a fulfilment of human hopes and aspirations, not by an escape from the world, but by its transfiguration into God. All shall share in that consummation; and our relation to it is determined by what we do now. We cannot imagine what this consummation will be like. But it is the consummation of what we now do, in its relation to God. Thus the

images of the great terrible Day of the Lord, and the
coming of the Son of Man in the power of the Spirit,
drawn from Daniel and the later prophets, are appropriate symbols for portraying to ourselves what the relation of our present life is to the goal of all things in
God. They speak of a future; but of a future which is a
completion and transfiguration of our present, seen in
its eternal perspective; not an endless continuation of
our commonplace lives, but the apotheosis of the temporal into the realm of the eternal.

So it is that Christian faith both emphasizes the
absoluteness and over-ridingness of ethical imperatives, as the demand of God himself, giving point and
purpose to our present lives. But it also reveals even
our greatest moral efforts as falling short of the ideal
of love. It is wholly understandable that Niebuhr
should term the moral teaching of Jesus an 'impossible possibility'. For Jesus shows what is ethically
demanded; but he also points to a dimension of love
which is beyond our moral striving and obedience, a
realm in the light of which we perceive that the sense
of duty is little more than the refraction of love into a
disfigured world. Jesus points to life in the Kingdom,
which can and will be realized in future; but which
can only be partially prefigured in this age. Because
our attempts to discern and respond to the love of
God are always partial and incomplete, we need to
know that we are accepted in love, despite our present
estrangement. Forgiveness is reconciliation to God,
and the promise of fulfilment hereafter. As Niebuhr
writes, 'Every one who rejects . . . the idea of the
resurrection is either a moral nihilist or an utopian.[22]
That is, either their awareness of the indifference of
the world to morality will lead to scepticism and an
undermining of moral effort and belief. Or they will
have to believe in the possibility of a future perfection
upon an unchanged earth – which will lead either to

sentimental and ineffective optimism or dangerous attempts to achieve Utopia by force. What Christian ethics offer, however, is the hope of moral fulfilment, even in the apparent reality of defeat.

What are the implications of this interpretation of Christian hope for the political ideals and principles of Christians? A Christian doctrine which calls us to love our fellows as ourselves and care for their needs must have a social and political dimension, as we work out how love can best be shown in societies for which we take responsibility. God has created human persons and placed them in societies. He wills that they should find there a proper fulfilment of the individual and social values inherent in that created structure. It is only reasonable to suppose that, if there are purposes to be achieved by historical existence, our actions should be at least partly governed by reference to those purposes. Christian eschatology is important, because it stands in opposition both to the view that there is no goal other than those we make up for ourselves; and to the view that there is a goal achievable by human effort.

In setting out his view, Niebuhr was, at least on occasions, perhaps a little unduly critical of the Christian traditions of Natural Law and of what he calls 'sacramentalism' in the Catholic streams of faith. He sometimes wrote that they sanctified a feudal natural order and destroyed prophetic moral judgements and interest in a dynamic future. But this is not necessarily, or even properly, the case. Natural law points to the sort of acts which realize the purposes of creation; and in placing this law above the law of any sovereign, it presents the possibility of a radical and revolutionary challenge to injustice and the status quo. Again, the sacraments do not mediate a sort of relaxing comfort, but the active love which is to transform the world to its proper destiny. The sort of religiosity which spiritualizes the idea of the Kingdom, making it a purely spiritual, inward, personal or other-worldly reality, is basically false to the biblical teaching that God intends to redeem the whole world, and calls us to share in his saving activity. A truly Catholic approach can hardly fail to stress the doctrine of Incarnation, which directly implies that the material, public world is to be taken up into the purposes of God, and indeed ultimately assumed into God himself, through the incarnate Word. Thus Christians are called to realize a social, political goal in history, to seek conditions in which every person can realize most fully their God-given capacities and inclinations. This is not a purpose we may or may not choose. It is set for us by the Creator himself, in the structure of creation.

On the other hand, a faith which is also founded on acceptance of a resurrection which comes by way of the cross and death cannot look for a natural and painless transition to the just society. The Kingdom will be realized; and it will be realized partly by what we do; yet it will not come by natural human contrivance. It is worth striving morally; for our actions will have an appropriate fulfilment. But that fulfilment will not be in 'this age', but in 'the age to come', the transfigured creation, at Christ's coming in glory. It is for this reason that Christian social action is not wholly dependent upon the calculation of actual consequences in our society. It cannot be undermined by worldly failure, and it should never be misled into claiming worldly success. The resolute action without anxious attachment for which Jesus calls (Matt. 6.25) is only possible when we accept in faith that our acts will find fulfilment, but do not look for that fulfilment in immediate social change. Christian eschatology requires us to measure our political acts by standards and norms higher than those of expediency or practicality; but none the less to seek to realize those stand-

ards as far as possible within the conditions and
constraints of our own time.

Christian social thought has tended to oscillate
between a radical pessimism that seeks only to save
the individual from the wrecks of time; and a triumphalist or radical optimism that expects good will and
correct belief to establish the Kingdom here and now.
The eschatalogical vision explored by Niebuhr rules
out both approaches. The eternal is expressed in the
temporal; and the temporal is fulfilled in the eternal.
In this double movement of expression and fulfilment
is to be found both the meaning and importance of
the historical and the placing of final fulfilment
beyond the historical. If we can have no hope for this
world, then the creation is in vain. But if our hope is
for this world only, then are we the most miserable of
beings.

One view that is ruled out is political quietism, the
acceptance of the *status quo* because no good can be
realized in the world at all. On the contrary, there is a
real and inescapable demand to realize the Kingdom
in history, to pursue the ideals of love and of what
Niebuhr calls 'equal justice'. The positive social ideals
of the gospel are those which enable natural human
gifts and inclinations to be realized equitably and in a
community of co-operation and justice. Distinguishing
features of such a society will be concern for the poor
and the weak, and respect for all human life, without
distinction of race, culture or achievement. It is a
Christian duty to seek to realize such a society, so far
as is possible in our situation.

On the other hand, any form of what may be called
'Liberal perfectionism' or Utopianism is also ruled out.
For sin always lies at the door, and self-interest will
never be finally defeated. Thus power will always cor-
rupt; and must always be subject to criticism and limitation. This makes any idea either of a 'Christian State'

or of a Marxist or Socialist State dangerous and unde-
sirable, since such ideas locate power too much in the
hands of powerful and uncriticizable central authorities. And it is even worse when those authorities
believe themselves to have a monopoly of right. Thus
political realism requires a system of checks and balances on power, and the maintenance of an order in
which people are free to pursue their own concerns,
unregulated by the vast plans of corporations or
councils.

What seems best to reflect Christian hope in political reality, then, is a sort of two-tier political ethic. The
first tier is that of justice, in the sense of negative
rights – refraining from interfering in the legitimate
plans and pursuits of others, and respecting their pursuits as part of respecting them, but also being prepared to prevent them from unduly obstructing the
legitimate plans of others. The second tier is that of
charity, of the pursuit of ideals of social self-
realization, which form the real vision and inspiration
of Christian social life. It is important to see, however,
that this second tier proposes a set of ideals which can
never be fully realized, whereas the first tier can and
should be implemented in any society. That does not
mean that the second tier is less important. In one
clear sense, it is the most important of all for a Christian. But it falls into the realm of the 'impossible possibility', the asymptotic ideal which it would be
mistaken ever to equate with any actual state of affairs.

It may be thought, and has sometimes been said,
that Niebuhr's views merely reflect the ideology of
American liberal democracy, with perhaps a tinge of
well-controlled radicalism. I think that this would be
unjust; and I have tried to show how they are rather
implicit in a particular, and persuasive, interpretation
of New Testament eschatology. The Christian hope
which is set before us in the teachings and in the life

of Christ requires us to commit ourselves positively to the social life of the world, without ever accepting its actual structures as satisfactory and without thinking that there is some perfect alternative. What it suggests is not a set of specific political doctrines – indeed, it rather suggests that there will be no unchanging or absolute set of particular principles, which will work in all societies. But it does set before us a vision and a perspective, a matrix within which our particular political views must be formed, out of our specific situation and society. It is not so much in the particular conclusions it provides, as in the personal working through and appropriation of the biblical symbolism in its application to our world which it exemplifies, that Niebuhr's political philosophy has much to teach. It will not dictate to us what we should think. But it will teach us how we can hold firmly to a Christian hope without despair and without naivety, in a world in which the Kingdom is always both 'now and not yet'.

NOTES

1. *An Interpretation of Christian Ethics*, p. 9.
2. *Beyond Tragedy.*
3. *The Nature and Destiny of Man* Vol. 2, p. 328.
4. *An Interpretation of Christian Ethics*, p. 60.
5. *The Nature and Destiny of Man*, Vol. 2, p. 83.
6. *An Interpretation of Christian Ethics*, p. 59.
7. *Beyond Tragedy*, p. 19.
8. *An Interpretation of Christian Ethics*, p. 188.
9. *The Nature and Destiny of Man*, Vol. 2, p. 305.
10. *The Nature and Destiny of Man*, Vol. 1, p. 285.
11. *The Nature and Destiny of Man*, Vol. 2, p. II.
12. *The Nature and Destiny of Man*, Vol. 2, p. 50.
13. *The Nature and Destiny of Man*, Vol. 2, p. 49.
14. *The Nature and Destiny of Man*, Vol. 2, p. 296.
15. *An Interpretation of Christian Ethics*, p. III.
16. *The Nature and Destiny of Man*, Vol. 2, p. 77.

17. *The Nature and Destiny of Man*, Vol. 2, p. 46.
18. *An Interpretation of Christian Ethics*, p. 36.
19. *The Nature and Destiny of Man*, Vol. 1, p. 189.
20. *The Nature and Destiny of Man*, Vol. 2, p. 188.
21. *Beyond Tragedy*, p. 302.
22. *Beyond Tragedy*, p. 305.

Reinhold Niebuhr and the New Right

RONALD PRESTON

Recently there was a popular BBC television comedy series, *Yes Minister*. Its two main characters were James Hacker, the Minister for Administrative Affairs, and his Civil Service Permanent Secretary, Sir Humphrey Appleby. The scripts were subsequently published as if they were extracts from Hacker's diary. In one of the scripts Hacker has discovered, through a private informant, that British-made bomb detonators have been sold through the arms trade and been secured by Italian terrorists. He regards it as a serious moral issue, and tells Appleby that he intends to inform the Prime Minister.

Appleby: 'Minister, Government isn't about morality.'

Hacker: 'Really? Then what is it about?'

Appleby: It's about stability. Keeping things going. Preventing anarchy. Stopping society falling to bits. Still being here tomorrow.'

Hacker: 'But what *for*?' I asked.

I had stumped him. He didn't understand my question. So I spelt it out for him.

'What is the ultimate purpose of Government if it isn't for doing good?' This notion was completely meaningless to him.

88

Appleby: 'Government isn't about good and evil, it's only about order and chaos.'[1]

This comedy series is a good introduction to the new, or radical, Right. It makes fun of amiable and ineffective 'do good' politicians, who, incidentally, lack the self-knowledge to realize the extent to which they are moved by their own desire for power (Niebuhr would have appreciated this). It also lampoons the Civil Service, whose main concern is to keep a smooth career structure ticking over for themselves. And this dialogue expresses a suspicion of anything but minimum government characteristic of the new Right. Part of the popularity of the series was due to the fact that it was in tune with one current mood in the UK, and it was no surprise to find Mrs Thatcher registering approval of it. But if some aspects would be congenial to Niebuhr, how far is it possible to enlist his support for the new Right? In examining this question I shall not deal with the entire conspectus of neo-conservatism, but confine myself to economic issues and the political ones to which they give rise.

Niebuhr died in 1971. His crucial work was done in the years 1932–52. He produced an immensely impressive political theology for his time. But times change. Indeed in his lifetime new theological strains were heard. There was, for instance, the theology of Hope, where Moltmann has been the outstanding name, and the theology of the Secular, chiefly in debt to Bonhoeffer. Then a new political theology developed in Europe, for instance by Metz; this has been criticized and carried further by the theologians of Liberation and of Revolution of Latin America. Anticipations of all these are found in Niebuhr, but they challenge his most characteristic stresses. Adherents of all of them tend to criticize him as being too much of an apologist for the American way of life, and too pessimistic about radical social change. For this reason he has seemed to fall out of favour. This often happens to leading thinkers for a period after their death. One reason is that universities at their best teach their students to develop their critical powers. The best students do this by sharpening their critical teeth on those who taught them and the authorities they recommended. (The camp followers just adopt the latest line and do not even read the works of those being displaced – they merely repeat criticisms of them.)

To some extent this has happened to Niebuhr, but by no means entirely. Interest in his thought has never ceased, and recently it has grown. Several of his books continue to appear on reading lists in political courses; and in theology my own University department has, since I retired, instituted a third year undergraduate option on Reinhold and Richard Niebuhr. It is not uncommon to find students who have been introduced to Reinhold Niebuhr filled with intellectual excitement that a flood of light is shed by him on the public issues of today. And in the realm of doctrinal studies it is interesting to note that the last chapter of Schubert Ogden's Sarum Lectures of 1982, on Christology, is dominated by Niebuhr.[2] However, in the political life of the USA and the UK a strange phenomenon has occurred. Right wing administrations have come to power with ideas which are a throwback to positions widely held fifty years ago, and, at least in the UK, more or less buried in between; and in some quarters Niebuhr has been enlisted as a supporter of them.

By the new, or radical, Right, I do not mean the 'Moral Majority' type of revivalist biblical fundamentalism which flourishes in the USA. I mean a recurrence of a free enterprise capitalist philosophy among circles much wider than the 'moral majority' folk. It is a com-

monplace that political parties are not monolithic entities, but include a wide spectrum of interests. In the
UK the Tory party has at least two main elements. One
is a more hierarchical, paternalist and organic outlook
with a sense of *noblesse oblige*. It is this which contributed the Tory element after 1945 in the consensus
politics behind the Welfare State, or what the Germans
call the social market economy. And it is this element
which is at present in eclipse; its opponents in the
Tory party have succeeded in fastening the pejorative
term 'wet' on to it. The other element in Toryism, akin
to Reaganism in the USA, is a return to the capitalist
philosophy of possessive individualism, involving minimum government, a free market economy and, wher-
ever possible, an appeal to private benevolence or
corporate voluntary effort where personal provisions
are not able to cope with personal misfortunes. This is
the new, or radical, Right. After years in the wilder-
ness, intellectual libertarianism has come to the fore,
and supporters of the mixed economy are in retreat. At
the same time supporters of a centralized socialist
economy are increasingly having to come to terms
with evidence of its inefficiency and oppression.

The basic assumption of the new Right is that
society, left to itself, has a 'natural' tendency to freedom, economic growth, and the removal of poverty.
By freedom is meant the narrow sense of the absence
of coercion by political power. Hence the new Right
holds that government should confine itself to little
more than the minimum task of safeguarding law and
order, the enforcement of contracts, and preservation
from aggression by other states. Extending government
activity beyond these merely interferes with 'natural'
tendencies. Governments are competent only in a
narrow area, and this does not include detailed man-
agement of the economy. If they are well-intentioned
in this area they are inefficient; but more often they

give way to special interest groups in the search for votes. In either case the coercive element, which is of the essence of government, is misused, if only because economic and political power is too concentrated. Politics becomes an unprincipled auction, with rival parties bribing the electorate with their economic policies, and the electors voting for diffuse and remote party platforms over which they have little check. How much better the precise, immediate, automatic operation of the free market, whose very impersonality is a blessing, since its outcome is the result of myriads of choices and cannot be laid at the door of any individual or group! By contrast, the result of politicizing so many economic issues is that governments promise what they cannot deliver, electorates become disillusioned with all parties, and the country is in danger of becoming ungovernable. In the inevitable trade-off between liberty, equality and fraternity, the new Right gives absolute priority to liberty.

If this were the occasion to comment at any length on the rival outlooks of those who support the Welfare State, and those who advocate a free market economy, it would be necessary to show that the supporters of each are often unrealistic. But the lack of realism of supporters of the Welfare State is as nothing compared with those of the free market. The latter show an extreme political naivety which overlooks the reality of private coercion – whether by firms, professional associations, or private networks – which only the state can hold in check. However, our concern is not to develop such a critique but to examine the relation of Niebuhr's thought to this economic outlook of the new Right.

In a recent review, Professor David Martin of the London School of Economics has remarked that Niebuhr is probably more quoted by apologists of the American way of life than by its critics.[3] If so, as we shall see, it is a case of being taken up by Conservatives who like what they think is his theology but not his politics, contrasted with liberals who for years have liked his politics but disliked his theology. A generation ago in the USA Russell Kirk, a neo-conservative, claimed support for what is usually called the 'realism' of Niebuhr. After remarking that the true conservative is a theist, and that the religious mind is at least conservative because it trusts in the wisdom of our ancestors, he goes on to say, 'Dr Reinhold Niebuhr's progress, in the course of a very few years, from a flirtation with "neutralism" to a forthright social conservatism is perhaps our best recent illustration of the bond between religious conviction and order in society'.[4] The 'realism' of Niebuhr is usually held to mean primarily his stress on Original Sin. He certainly did stress it; and the fact that in his later writings he abandoned the term because it was always misunderstood does not affect the point that it was the reality of the phenomenon not the name given to it with which he was concerned.[5] However, the neo-conservative stress on Niebuhr's teaching on Original Sin is too simple, both in the lessons it draws from it, and by overlooking the equally significant balancing element in his thought, Original Righteousness. I shall return to this point. Meanwhile, it should be noted that Russell Kirk's reference to Niebuhr's social conservatism refers to a greater appreciation in his writings of the organic elements in society. Niebuhr said of this that it related to an increasing appreciation by him, 'of the organic factors in social life in contrast to tendencies stemming from the Enlightenment'. However, this does not support the individualistic outlook of the new Right of today. Indeed he called the neo-conservatism of Kirk nothing more than a decadent liberalism, in practice too interested in preserving the *status quo*, something which he said is anathema to anyone who has drawn inspiration from the Old Testament prophets.[6]   I shall also return to the organic element in Niebuhr's thought.

Moving to contemporary discussions, two authors who have recently claimed the support of Niebuhr for the new Right are the Lutheran, Robert Benne, and the Roman Catholic, Michael Novak. Benne maintains in the Preface to his *The Ethics of Democratic Capitalism* that the whole book is an attempt to bring a Niebuhrian approach, which he outlines at the beginning, to bear on a reasoned – but not entirely uncritical – defence of the current American version of capitalism. In the event, attention to Niebuhr's thought fades as the book proceeds, and it is not brought to bear on the various features of capitalism which are discussed. Benne's main point is that insistence that the seat of sin does not reside in the external conditions of society, but in the human heart, leads to the desirability of a capitalist economy, because it leads to the diffusing rather than the concentration of power. Another beneficent effect of stressing the Fall, though Benne does not do this directly, is to say that the private property and inequality which are due to it are also a divine contrivance for bringing out in the economic order their best efforts from people; and that capitalism expresses this divine intention by harnessing self-interest to promote efficiency and economic growth, which benefits everyone.[8]

Novak, however, is more detailed than Benne in harnessing Niebuhr to the market economy. His *The Spirit of Democratic Capitalism* has a whole chapter on him, and many other references in addition.[9] Novak maintains that in 1952 in *The Irony of American History*, Niebuhr blazed a trail which should have culminated in a new vision of the American economic system as a form of political economy most consonant with the Judaic tradition and the Christian gospel. But he stopped short of doing so. Novak's contention appears to be based on Niebuhr's alleged view that the American *experience* of democratic capitalism is better than the *theory* of it. This is based on a sentence at the beginning of chapter 5, which says America's successful social and political policies have frequently defied its social creed; an ironic form of success (as he remarks), and a frail basis for Novak to build on. Novak also quotes from the same book Niebuhr's remark, 'There are elements of truth . . . in classical economies which remain a permanent treasure of a free society, since some forms of a "free market" are essential to democracy. The alternative is the regulation of economic process through bureaucratic-political decisions. Such regulation, too consistently applied, involves the final peril of combining political and economic power.'[10] However, the phrase 'some forms of a free market' in the quotation hides all the problems at issue in the struggle to find in the area of social democracy and democratic socialism an economic order which is both efficient and humane. We must never allow ourselves to assume we are confined to two 'ideal' alternatives (to use a term from Max Weber), a completely free market or a totally centrally planned economy. There are issues here which press upon us with great urgency. Niebuhr did not give much attention to them; his interests were focused more politically than economically.[11] His preoccupations were increasingly with foreign and global affairs. In economic matters he seems to have stayed with the conviction that the mixed economy had solved basic economic problems in principle by incorporating non-capitalist elements which made capitalism tolerable. But, as indeed Novak points out, he never took back his criticisms of dangerous concentrations of power in practice if the free market is left entirely to itself, nor did he withdraw his criticisms, in the light of man's social nature, of individualism as a philosophy.[12]

Novak's thinking assumes that political democracy, a market economy, and free enterprise go together. Since Niebuhr was an outstanding theological defender of a 'western' type of political democracy, as the best method of finding proximate solutions to insoluble problems, it is assumed, too readily, that he can be roped in too unqualifiedly to support the free market.[13] Novak is one of the founders of the Institute for Religion and Democracy, which in 1981 issued a statement on 'Christianity and Democracy'. Among many well taken points, it associates political demo-cracy with a free market, and the USA as a standard-bearer of both, in a way which Niebuhr would have qualified drastically.

To return to the question of Original Sin. Niebuhr first became known as a critic of an evolutionary optimism which was a characteristic expression of American culture in the 1920s, and whose theological expression was found in the Social Gospel. Dismissive adjectives on both stand out in his writings: sentimen-tal, idealistic, utopian, unrealistic, perfectionist. He held that they showed an excessive reliance on ration-ally designed plans, too great a readiness to manipu-late human beings, too cavalier an attitude to immediate means in pursuing desirable collective ends, and a self-deception as to their own motives by exponents of these stances, notably a love of exercis-ing power. That was why he thought it was necessary to move theologically to the right and politically to the left. Hence the stress on Original Sin. But it was not long before he gave attention to Original Righteous-ness. It was this that led to a greater emphasis on the organic elements in human society and culture; it stemmed from a greater appreciation of common grace, no longer distinguished so sharply from saving

REINHOLD NIEBUHR AND THE NEW RIGHT   97

grace. This led to an increasing respect for the thought of Edmund Burke. It is this which makes him congenial to Tory 'wets', but it is very far from the individualism of the Tory radical Right.

This greater appreciation of the organic side of conservatism can therefore be passed over quickly because it is not the focus of the new Right. In *The Self and the Dramas of History* he warns against ignoring the organic factors in society, including social stratification and property as sources of social cohesion, rather than relying on an abstract liberal reformism. One of his criticisms of the new Right would be, in fact, that it lacks a feeling for the social substance of human existence.[14]

In spite of this criticism he had, as we have seen, favourable things to say about the free market. He expressed appreciation of the Puritan ethic of thrift, diligence and honesty, which is the best theological contribution to it, provided it was not mixed with a callow Social Darwinism.[15] His most sustained treatment of it is his chapter on 'The Christian Faith and the Economic Life of Liberal Society' in an enquiry sponsored by the American Federal Council of Churches in 1953.[16] He says that the achievement of economic liberalism was the doctrine that, 'the vast system of mutual service which constitutes the life of economic society could best be maintained by relying on the "self-interest" of men rather than their "benevolence" or on moral persuasion, or by freeing economic activity from irrelevant and frequently undue restrictive political controls.' It also made secular ends genuinely respectable, as against a pseudo otherworldliness, or the premature sanctification of institutions in traditional societies. But he denies that the operation of the market will produce an automatic harmony, as liberals assume, because it ignores the factor of power, the social function of property, and the collective production of wealth; it also equates every form of self-interest with economic interest, ignoring, for example, ethnic and national loyalties, and the desire to play, to love, and to dominate. Nevertheless, he is sure that self-interest must be harnessed to economic processes, contrary to the simplicities of much socialist thought, because of concern for one's family, and because no one in society is good enough or wise enough finally to determine how an individual's capacities may best be used for the common good.[17] We need to preserve self-regulating forces in the economic process, otherwise the task of control becomes too stupendous and endangers liberty.[18] However, this does not alter the fact that relative justice is likely to be with the radical Left because the Right has more power, as well as the force of inertia, on its side.

Niebuhr has a chapter on 'The Brief Glory of the Business Man' in *Reflections on the End of an Era*, and three more chapters in the same book on individualism.[19] He says that the hegemony of the business man may last another hundred years, but that will give him only two hundred years in all, since it was not until the mid-nineteenth century that he had dissolved the old social relations, thus obscuring the human factor and dissolving the complexities of social relations in a control by the mechanisms of commercial exchange. There is now no *noblesse oblige*. Quoting de Tocqueville that 'power alone cannot maintain itself where reverence is lacking', Niebuhr says that captains of industry were never really captains in that they could not be symbols of unity, they could not elaborate an effective ritual, and they could not conceal their class interests behind common hopes and fears. They could be successful as entrepreneurs but could not inspire reverence. 'A mechanical society collapses more quickly than an organic one when its day is done.'

By contrast the new Right has an optimistic view of the future if economic processes are left to the automatic devices of the market uncorrupted by politics. Many thinkers, both religious and secular, have pointed out that capitalism is underpinned by moral commitments of which it is unaware, and undermines rather than promotes. I do not think Niebuhr addressed himself to this point so specifically. He did, however, have his own provisional optimism about the human future, but it was not based on the negative view of politics of the new Right. In addition to the chapter on Original Righteousness in the first volume of the Gifford Lectures, the second volume is largely devoted to the need for a synthesis of Reformation and Renaissance outlooks.[20] For one thing the Renaissance had shown an awareness of the provisional autonomy of secular disciplines, and that evidence from these is necessary to examine the current situation in an effort to understand 'what is going on' (to borrow a phrase from Richard Niebuhr), and to arrive at proximate norms for the direction of policy. Christian discernment springs from insights from the Gospels, the experience of secular disciplines (which have some technical aspects where the church has no special competence), and common sense.[21] There are important issues here which Niebuhr never expanded, and which I have dealt with elsewhere.[22] Further, he has what to many are surprising affirmations about historical possibilities. History has endless possibilities of good as well as of evil. It moves forward to more inclusive ends. The possibilities for the future are wholly indeterminate. 'Wholly' is a dangerously unambiguous term for Niebuhr to use. Nevertheless there will always be ambiguities because it is the very greatness of human beings which makes possible the depths of sin. In the chapter on 'The Kingdom of God and the Struggle for Justice' in volume two he says,

'There are no limits to be set in history for the achievement of more universal human brotherhood, for the development of more perfect and more inclusive human relations'.[23] It is because of an understanding of common grace that we can draw upon a moral wisdom that is not dependent upon the Judaeo-Christian tradition. Hence piecemeal claims for justice can be widely heard and elicit some response.

Niebuhr was open to the good in human persons, especially to those who have no moral pretensions. Indeed his realism led him to maintain that structures of justice are necessary partly as a protection against the paternalism of love. They are also necessary because the comfortable do not take seriously the burden of injustice until its victims begin to gain countervailing power. That is why it is so unconvincing to ally him with the political Right. He was well aware that the hitherto powerless will misuse power when they gain it unless there are institutional checks to restrain them, which is why he was a political democrat. But he would have little sympathy with the new Right. He was clear that his 'realistic' conception of human nature was not to be made the bastion of a conservatism which defended unjust privilege, but that it must be the servant of an ethic of social justice.

In this task he wanted the Christian faith to be a source of discernment and not fanaticism. It can be argued that he preserved every proper claim and hope for the created world, and that he put forward a better political theology than has subsequently been adumbrated. He realized the need for vision and for hope, and he saw the need to be free from the fear of making mistakes, or the illusion in a question for perfection that it might be possible never to make one. He maintained the need for a Christian commitment to social justice in full awareness of the complexities involved. He stood for a hope the other side of pessimism.

Does it work out like that? Christians do not find it easy to hold to Niebuhr's subtle balance in both thought and practice. The danger of eschatological reserve can easily stultify commitment and turn us into indecisive Hamlets, unable to make up our minds or to persist in pursuing relative goals. However the corruptions of a doctrine are not evidence against it if they are specifically repudiated by it. More serious is the charge that the realism of Niebuhr, with its accompanying 'pragmatism' in respect of immediate decisions is in fact a conservative stance, because in asking 'What works?' it does so within an existing functioning social system, and presupposes too much of a general consensus with respect to it.[24] Should not our imaginations burst the bounds of the existing order? If no one tries for the impossible how shall we know the limits of the possible? Theologies of Hope have stressed the need to expect new things from God, an *advent*, not a calculable future based on extrapolations from present trends, which is an inherently conservative activity; they have stressed the heralding of the creatively unexpected which does not arise out of the past. The resurrection of Christ is the paradigm. This is heady doctrine. It leads to a welcome openness of spirit. But it does not provide any basis for decisions which go on having to be made in the present. In practice it seems to lead to 'progressive' choices, often made on the basis of somewhat slipshod analyses, which are apt to follow without sufficient critical scrutiny those current in 'progressive' circles at the time. To Niebuhr, pragmatism meant a steady commitment to social justice in full recognition of the complexities involved.

The upshot of our discussion is that the economic ideas of the new Right contain nothing new. They are the resurrection of notions which were current in the

1920s, and falsified in the years following the Wall
Street crash of 1929. Since we know what Niebuhr said
of them before, it is not hard to see what he would
say of them now. The element of truth in them is far
outweighed by their falsity. The new Right attitude is
'unnuanced', to use a term from John Bennett, in a
way quite foreign to Niebuhr's thought. He would
agree that the free market is a 'serviceable drudge', a
phrase used by R.H. Tawney of the state, if freed from
the dangerous philosophy of possessive individualism.
He would vindicate the realm of politics as against its
denigration by the radical Right. If the doctrine of
Original Sin stresses the imperfections of politics, that
of Original Righteousness indicates its necessity and
possibilities. In any event we are left with a host of
detailed economic problems, as the advanced industrial countries move rapidly into a third industrial
revolution whilst two-thirds of the world is embroiled
in rapid social changes brought about by the backwash
of the first two. We need Niebuhr's approach to face
these problems, but we cannot expect to draw from
him the precise policies we need.

Economic issues inevitably lead into political ones.
A better political theology is to be found based on
Niebuhr's eschatological critique of the *status quo*,
itself drawn from the element of realized eschatology
in the gospels, than any other on offer. It tackles the
relative judgements of the present with a hopefulness
for an open future, with all its possibilities and ambiguities, aware that there will be no final victory of the
righteous over the unrighteous in history, if only
because there are no simply righteous, not even the
oppressed. History must be fulfilled beyond history.
These thoughts are beyond the horizons of the new
Right; but it is no more plausible for them to harness
the thoughts of Reinhold Niebuhr at the terrestrial
ideological level at which they operate.

NOTES

Where the place of publication of books is not mentioned, it is London.

1. *Yes Minister,* Jonathan Lynn and Antony Jay, Vol. 3 (p. 116), BBC.
2. *The Point of Christology,* 1982.
3. *Times Literary Supplement.* Dec. 12, 1984 (p. 1341).
4. *A Programme for Conservatives,* Chicago, 1954 (p. 100).
5. See *Man's Nature and His Communities* (pp. 15ff). Peter Steinfels also refers to this time when writing of a group of intellectuals in the USA., the American Committee for Cultural Freedom, formed in 1951 to oppose all forms of thought control; he says that the neo-orthodox realism of Niebuhr linked the group to the religious world. *The Neo-Conservatives,* New York, 1979 (p. 29).
6. cf his 'Reply to Interpretations and Criticisms', in *Reinhold Niebuhr: His Religious, Social and Political Thought,* ed. C.W. Kegley and R.W. Brettall, New York, 1956 (p. 434); also quotations from him in John C. Bennett's essay in the same volume, 'Reinhold Niebuhr's Social Ethics' (p. 77). A new edition of this symposium, with additional material and assessments was published by the Pilgrim Press, New York in 1982, ed. C.W. Kegley.
7. Fortress Press, Philadelphia, 1981. He says in his Preface that Niebuhr has provided the formative notions of his philosophy and ethical position.
8. This was argued by the 'Christian Political Economists' in the UK in the period roughly 1800–1835. See Chapter 3, Section 1 of my Scott Holland Lectures, *Church and Society in the Late Twentieth Century,* 1983.
9. Simon and Schuster and the American Enterprise Institute, 1981, chap. 19. It is also entitled, 'From Marxism to Democratic Capitalism', both terms too unqualified as applied to Niebuhr. See the article, 'Niebuhr's Ethic: the later years', by John C. Bennett, the most authoritative interpreter of Niebuhr, in *Christianity and Crisis,* April 12, 1982. He quotes an article by Niebuhr in *The New Leader* of Dec. 23, 1957 as summarizing his basic position on economic issues. 'Adam Smith contributed mightily to a free society, but he almost wrecked that society with the unfulfilled promise that justice would flow inevitably from freedom. Karl Marx contributed mightily to a just society by his practical understanding of the realities of power in an industrial age, but he laid the foundations for a new despotism by not understanding these realities well enough. Fortunately we are living in a day in which healthy nations do not concern themselves too much with the dogmas of either Smith or Marx but profit by the truths that they have winnowed from the errors of both.' Niebuhr could not have written the last sentence today; the new Right is a throwback to what he thought we had outgrown.

    In the same article Bennett adds that there is no reason to suppose that Niebuhr ever ceased to believe in equality as a regulative principle by which all economic structures should be judged.

I am much indebted to John Bennett for copies of articles not easily accessible in the UK.

10. p. 93.

11. Chapter 8, on economic affairs in Gordon Harland's book, *The Thought of Reinhold Niebuhr*, New York, 1960, is slight by comparison with most of the rest of the book, and so is chapter 18, 'The Problem of Economic Power', in *Reinhold Niebuhr on Politics*, ed. Harry R. Davis and Robert C. Good, New York, 1960. Both books are thorough studies; the relative slightness of these chapters is due to the relative lack of material.

12. p. 329. Novak's otherwise well balanced chapter concludes, however, with assertions which do not follow from what has gone before, and which are an indication of an intellectual climate produced by the Reagan Presidency rather than for any bearing they have on Niebuhr. Novak says that Niebuhr is needed today to expose those who (1) uncritically accept the Third World as a Messianic force; (2) discount the military threat to the West by an armed force greater than Hitler; (3) resume again the attacks of the 1930s on concentrations of power in multi-national corporations.

13. See especially, *The Children of Light and the Children of Darkness*, and compare his 'Biblical Faith and Socialism', in *Religion and Culture: Essays in Honour of Paul Tillich*, ed. W. Leibrecht (1958).

14. 1956. cf. chapter 22.

15. *Christian Realism and Political Problems* (p. 66).

16. *Goals of Economic Life*, ed. A. Dudley Ward, New York, 1953 (p. 433).

17. Summarizing especially pp. 433–35 and 441–47.

18. See chap. 3, 'The Community and Property', in *The Children of Light and the Children of Darkness*.

19. 1934. Chapter 5. See also chaps. 7, 8 and 9.

20. *The Nature and Destiny of Man*, Vol. I, chap. 10, and *The Nature and Destiny of Man*, Vol. II, chaps. 3, 6, 7 and 9.

21. 'The Quality of our Lives', article in *The Christian Century*, May 4, 1960.

22. See Appendix 2 of my Scott Holland Lectures (note 8 *supra*).

23. *The Nature and Destiny of Man*, Vol. II, p. 89.

24. This is well discussed by Roger Shinn in an article, 'Realism, Radicalism and Eschatology in Reinhold Niebuhr: a Re-Assessment', in the *Journal of Religion*, Chicago, Oct. 1974.

25. In the article referred to in note 9 *supra*.

Reinhold Niebuhr's Critique of Pacifism and his Pacifist Critics

RICHARD HARRIES

Reinhold Niebuhr had great admiration for the type of non-violent resistance practised by Gandhi. He believed that it had moral strengths[1] and that it was a particularly strategic instrument for an oppressed minority group. In 1932 he predicted, 'The emancipation of the Negro race in America probably waits upon the adequate development of this kind of social and political strategy'.[2] Furthermore, he thought that religion had a particular contribution to make to the development of this type of resistance.[3]

Niebuhr's positive evaluation of the techniques of non-violent resistance should not be overlooked. Nevertheless, he strongly objected to two confusions that had grown up around it. First, in his judgement, Jesus taught total non-resistance, rather than non-violent resistance.[4] Secondly, he denied that there was an absolute moral distinction between the use of force and the techniques of non-violent resistance. He noted that Gandhi's boycott of English cotton resulted in the undernourishment of the children of Manchester and the Allied blockade of Germany in the death of German children.[5] So instead of the terms 'force' and 'non-violent resistance', he preferred to distinguish between violent and non-violent coercion. Both were forms of coercion: and we need our eyes open to the way that coercion, particularly economic coercion, is already operative in society, and working to the

benefit of the advantaged. Moreover, the attempt to
make an absolute distinction led to the absurd position that the non-violent power of Dr Goebbel's propaganda was more moral than the military efforts of
the Allies to resist Nazi tyranny.[6] So Niebuhr made two
basic distinctions. First, between *non*-resistance and all
forms of *resistance* and then between violent and non-
violent coercion.[7]

More recently Ronald Sider and Richard Taylor have
made a basic distinction between non-violent coercion
and what they call 'lethal violence'.[8] They maintain
that coercion is quite compatible with love and
instance the disciplining of children and the use of
economic boycotts. These forms of coercion, they say,
still respect 'the other person's freedom to say no and
accept the consequences'. Lethal violence on the other
hand is different, for then 'one cannot lovingly appeal
to the other person as a free moral agent responsible
to God to choose to repent and change'. As they write,
'It makes no sense to call a person to repentance as
you put a bullet through his head'. Sider and Taylor's
analysis is, however, confused. Consider three conditional sentences.

(1) If you don't stop bullying your sister you will go
    to your room.
(2) If you don't stop bullying your sister I will shoot
    you.
(3) If you don't drop your gun I'll shoot it out of
    your hand.

The fundamental distinction is *not* between the first
sentence and the other two, in both of which weapons
are mentioned, but between (2) on the one hand and
(1) and (3) on the other. The difference is that the
coercion in (1) and (3) are proportionate whilst that
in (2) is totally disproportionate. If a man is holding
up a bank and the police burst in and tell him to drop
his gun, their threat is the appropriate and proportion-

ate response to the threat posed. It is the minimum use of coercion necessary to achieve a legitimate goal.

Did Jesus resist evil? Sider and Taylor, unconsciously following Augustine, point to Jesus' verbal denunciation of the Pharisees, his cleaning of the Temple and his remark at the trial when a soldier struck him, 'If I have spoken wrongly, bear witness to the wrong: but if I have spoken rightly, why do you strike me?[9] They then argue that Christians *should* resist whilst at the same time being willing to suffer in the process. For loving means having 'the needs – not necessarily the wants' of the enemy in mind. This point, also made by Augustine in his commentary on the Sermon on the Mount, is surely correct. There is nothing worse for the aggressor than to allow him to get away with his aggression, for this simply reinforces the harmful tendency within him. For his own good, for the love of him, he has to be stopped. Sider and Taylor also admit that it is sometimes in the interest of the careless debtor to take him to court. So the authors are prepared to countenance the use of coercion. They maintain that discipline and boycotts are compatible both with the teaching of Jesus and the nature of love. They support disciplinary punishment (though not retributive punishment, which has to be left to God). They uphold the police and the courts, disassociating themselves from Tolstoy in this respect. They admire the British tradition of unarmed police and write: 'We would favour creative efforts to expand the many ways that police can use non-lethal coercion'.[10] So do we all of course – but the crucial question – which they dodge – is what happens if the criminal is armed and refuses to give up his arms? They slip away with the remark: 'In any case, police work is radically different from warfare'. Is it? It is a question that will be considered later. But what their previous argument amounts to is that coercive resistance is compatible with love –

up to a point. But what happens at that point – when a criminal refuses to give up his gun – we are not told.

There is, however, a question which Sider and Taylor do force the Niebuhrian to face. Is it possible to love someone at the same time as you put a bullet through their head? Leaving aside all other considerations, for example, weighing the life of the torturer against the person he is torturing, and considering only the enemy *per se*, is it possible to shoot and love at the same time? One possible answer is to say that you are not shooting to kill. Your prime intention is to render the attacker harmless, to disable him, and this is so whether the enemy is a terrorist or a soldier. However, it may be pressing the principle of double effect further than it will go to say that killing is an unintended result in every instance. There *is* an important distinction between what is directly intended and what is foreseen but unintended. Nevertheless, in some instances, killing is so inevitable that it probably cannot be regarded as unintended in terms of the action involved. Another possible answer is that just because a person is dead you do not have to cease loving him. On a Christian view personal identity exists beyond death, in God. So it is possible to continue to wish a person well and to pray for them. Sider and Taylor define their concept of love in terms of giving the person opportunity to repent on this earth. Some of us, however, would not care to limit God's action and our opportunity to repent, to this life. Bringing in the concept of everlasting life is dangerous. It could make us less sensitive to the deaths of others. Nevertheless, on a Christian view, it is difficult to see how it can be entirely left out of account. For if to love someone is to desire their good, their good in a Christian sense is not simply their good in community on this earth but eternal happiness in the Communion of Saints. Indeed, is it not true that to deny the

possibility of shooting at someone and loving them at
the same time is to deny the possibility of redemption? Someone becomes deranged and picks up a
hand grenade to throw into a school playground full
of children. Before he can throw it a policeman shoots
at him, severely disabling but not killing him. In
prison afterwards the person comes to his senses and
is glad that he was shot at, glad that he was prevented
from killing the children. He is glad too for his own
sake. He would not like to live forever with the
thought of having murdered innocent young lives.
Although it is foolish to speculate on what might
happen after death it must, on a Christian view, at
least be a place where people come to their senses
and see things as they are. Ultimate reconciliation
depends, for example, on the soldiers in Hitler's
armies, who were killed in battle, coming to see that it
was good they were stopped, even though it meant
their own death. Of course, in the heat of the battle
these considerations are unlikely to be present. But
the principle holds. To deny that it is possible to love
and shoot at the same time is to deny the possibility
of ultimate reconciliation.[11]

According to Niebuhr, Jesus taught total non-
resistance. But is the term 'non-resistance' an accurate
one to describe the impact of the kingdom of God
and what it asks of us? Every line of the Gospels wit-
nesses to God's resistance to evil in all its forms, a
resistance expressed through casting out devils, healing the sick and exposing hypocrisy. Indeed, total
non-resistance would be non-existence. To exist at all
is to exist with a life of one's own; a life which partly
defines itself in opposition to its surroundings.

A different terminology is needed to describe the
character of Jesus' actions and I prefer the phrase
'non-coercive resistance'. The Term 'non-resistance'
originally had a fairly clear meaning – it meant not

resisting physically, particularly not taking up arms against the sacred person of the monarch. But as a phrase it has now become confused and confusing. The NT puts before us a figure who resisted with all the power of his person, his words and his prayers. For the sake of clarity therefore, we need more distinctions than Sider and Taylor allow and a different terminology from that of Niebuhr. In addition to total non-resistance, which was not taught by Jesus, there are these categories of resistance.

(1) Non-coercive resistance that relies only on persuasion.
(2) Resistance that uses direct force, or the threat of force.
(3) Resistance that uses indirect coercion, through such means as strikes and boycotts.

There are significant differences between all three but the fundamental distinction must be between a resistance that relies on persuasion alone and that which makes use of either direct or indirect coercion. It is clearly confusing, if not hypocritical, as Niebuhr pointed out, to claim the moral aura that might be held to belong to non-coercive resistance whilst in fact making use of indirect coercion.[12]

As is well known, Niebuhr criticized pacifists for an over-optimistic view of man and for failing to take the presence of sin seriously enough. This was part of this wider critique of liberalism and his exposure of hidden liberal assumptions in avowedly Christian claims. In his book, *The Relevance of the Impossible: A Reply to Reinhold Niebuhr*,[13] first published in 1941, G.H.C. MacGregor made a point, which he repeated in 1953, and which has been followed by the many pacifists since then who have acknowledged their debt to this book. MacGregor argued that the Gospels do indeed see an essential, hidden goodness in the heart of man. Yet Niebuhr never denied man's capacity for justice. He simply urged that his inclination to injustice must *also* be taken into account. However much we may appeal to the hidden goodness in man, there is one inescapable fact. Christ was crucified. 'Though Christ is the true norm for every man, every man is also in some sense a crucifier of Christ.'[14] Sider and Taylor, in response to the criticism that pacifism reflects non-Christian liberal assumptions, point out that Mennonites hold to mainstream, orthodox beliefs on the incarnation, and the atonement; that there is no necessary connection between pacifism and liberalism and that though humanity is indeed sinful a new age has dawned and the spirit-filled Church has come into being. The same points are made by MacGregor and others. They argue that Niebuhr had no real sense of the Church, an inadequate grasp of the Holy Spirit and an undue emphasis on pardoning as opposed to enabling grace. They believe that within the spirit-filled Church, which is universal, there is grace and power to overcome the sin of man and to enable us to live out the commands of Christ.[15]

Suppose, however, this criticism is admitted – what are its implications? We have a fellowship, a spirit-filled community, universal in scope, capable of raising the standard of individual behaviour and of obeying the most severe requirements of Jesus; capable of living out his spirit-filled life of love both within the community and the world. Suppose we grant all this: what follows? Must not a Christian withdraw, in some significant sense, from public office: and the Church decisively separate itself from national life? John Yoder, after analysing some of the twenty-five types of pacifism which he identifies, comes to his own form, which he calls 'the pacifism of the messianic community'.[16] This pacifism is messianic because it depends upon the confession that Jesus is Christ and Lord and it is Christocentric in that it is based on the assumption that God has been revealed in Christ. It is also a pacifism of the community. It is not simply for heroic individuals but for a community that experiences in its life a foretaste of God's kingdom. It is a community dedicated to a deviant value system and empowered by the Spirit which is changing the world.

This is a magnificent vision of the Church. But how does it bear on those of its members who are serving in public life? For those in office have a duty to preserve, and make to flourish, the body for which they have a responsibility. We do not commend deans of science faculties who give away all their science equipment to needier universities or bank managers who give away their bank funds. Public policy is based upon the assumption that there is a legitimate self-interest to be protected. It is difficult to see how a Christian, on Yoder's view, can have any part in it. Older forms of pacifism of the Mennonite type surmounted this difficulty by frank acknowledgement of the need to withdraw from society. The new pacifism does not wish to follow this path. Yoder believes that Christ's uncompromising demands are directed to all men.[17] Sider and Taylor, too, explicitly reject all forms of dualism. They write:

> We do not believe God has a double ethic. We do not believe God ordains a higher ethic for especially devout folk and a lower ethic for the masses. We do not believe that God intends Christians to wait until the millennium to obey the Sermon on the Mount. We do not believe God commands one thing for the individual and another for that same person as a public official.[18]

There is not space to reflect on all these different expressions of dualism. There is one fundamental point, however, upon which all forms of ethical dualism rest, which is crucial to Niebuhr and to the Christian faith. At the Eucharist Christians acclaim 'Christ has died, Christ is risen, Christ will come again'. The Christian Church lives between the times, between Christ risen and Christ coming again. This tension is part of its life and any attempt to collapse it by denying one of the poles inevitably gives rise to distortions.

Niebuhr argued that you cannot understand the ethical teaching of Christ without taking into account the eschatological dimension.

> The ethical demands made by Jesus are incapable of fulfilment in the present existence of man. They proceed from a transcendent and divine unity of essential reality, and their final fulfilment is possible only when God transmutes the present chaos of this world into its final unity.[19]

In other words, in this world morally right action does not guarantee a happy outcome. On the contrary, good people often suffer for their goodness. It is only in the Kingdom that the universe will be totally transparent to value.

Niebuhr rejected the idea that we have to wait for Kingdom come before experiencing the claims of its ethic. On the contrary it bears upon us now and it bears upon *every* aspect of our life, public as well as private. Nevertheless, there is a fundamental contrast between what is possible in the fullness of the Kingdom and what is possible now. There is a difference between the ethic of the Kingdom of God, 'in which no concession is made to human sin, and all relative political strategies which, assuming human sinfulness, seek to secure the highest measure of peace and justice among selfish and sinful men'.[20] There is then a tension that is basic to the Christian life because the church lives between Christ risen and Christ coming again. The denial by pacifists of all forms of dualism is in effect a repudiation of this tension. As MacGregor writes:

> Christian pacifists have often been warned by self-styled 'realists' that we shall never bring in the Kingdom of God by acting in an evil world as if it were already here. Yet this is, I suggest, exactly what Jesus *did* teach: if only men were prepared to take God at his word and to order their lives here and now by the laws of a transcendent Kingdom, then the power of God would answer the cry of faith, and the Kingdom would break in upon them unawares.[21]

This is well said and it places the claims of Jesus squarely before us. Moreover, as Niebuhr's critics rightly urge, the presence of sin in human life in no way lessens the claim of his ethical teaching upon us. Sin or no we are called to respond as best we can. However, if we do act in an evil world as if the Kingdom of God were here, we must reckon with the possibility of failure. Christ was crucified and the disciple is not above his master. This point, which is not always grasped, has crucial implications. First, the way of self-sacrifice has to be personally chosen. It cannot be imposed. The individual Christian can choose this path and so can the Church: but can a nation? MacGregor quoted Dean Inge with approval, 'The notion of a martyr-nation, giving itself up to injustice and spoilation for the most sacred of all causes, cannot be dismissed with contempt'.[22] Sider and Taylor make the same point:

> We can imagine America's leaders saying to the aggressor: 'You can create scorched earth and dead cities, but you cannot make us give in to tyranny. You can kill the innocent, but their blood will cry out against you; and God will hear.'[23]

In these assertions there is an illegitimate comparison between a Church, which might be called upon to choose martyrdom rather than defend itself and a nation handed over to tyranny by leaders elected to office precisely in order not to get the nation into a situation where the only choice was one of submission to tyranny or mutual annihilation. This is not to deny that many nations now and in the past have had to suffer silently rather than resist by force because that has been the least destructive course of action open to them. But that is very different from leaders, responsible for the safety of their people, letting them slip into that position when other alternatives are open to them.

Yet Christ is risen. The cross is only half the story. Perhaps we should ask a nation to walk the way of martyrdom in the hope that God will validate those who obey his commands? But we cannot predict when or how Resurrection victory will be shown. Christ died with a mixture of despair, trust and hope. He did not go to the cross in the certainty that this was a tunnel through to resurrection on the third day. Christian hope gives rise to policies but is not itself a policy. Politics, on the other hand, works by calculation. Luther said he would rather have as ruler a bad man who was prudent than a good man who was imprudent. Prudence, that is, trying carefully to assess the consequences of our actions and to weigh them in the light of all the factors, is what politics is about. Christian hope is not a form of prudence.

The implications of this must not be avoided. The way of the cross can be chosen by an individual or by a Christian community. It can hardly be chosen by rulers for a nation as a whole. It is difficult to see how Christian pacifists of this ilk can in conscience hold public office.

Does God will, or not will, human communities to continue? There are three points to be made. First, 'mind', as Austin Farrer used to say, 'is a social reality'. There cannot be such a thing as a totally isolated individual. We were all once talked into talking and thinking by others. There can be no human personality without human community. Secondly, human communities more advanced than that of the Stone Age require a political centre. They are political communities. Thirdly, although it is natural, as Aquinas said, for human beings to come together, because we are social beings, we can only stay together in a fallen world with a degree of coercion.

The conclusion must be that so long as God wills human life to continue he wills political communities and the means without which they cannot exist. It is therefore our responsibility to operate those mechanisms without which there can be no community. To think that human community can exist without some coercion is again to think that the Kingdom has come in its fullness.

Some modern pacifists allow coercion up to a point; they also allow justice as an independent norm up to a point but only within the state, not in the states system as a whole. Niebuhr was more consistent. He came at his consideration of justice through the social struggle and it was the same justice he was concerned to see implemented in the International order. The power of the strong over the weak, the tendency of the mighty to tyrannize the powerless, had to be checked both within the state and between states. The difficulty of looking for justice in the states system is obvious. There is no central authority with power to enforce its own decisions. Each nation has to act as advocate, judge and law enforcement officer in its own cause. The likelihood for self-interest here, the boundless capacity of people to deceive themselves and the scope with modern propaganda methods for governments to deceive their people, makes us highly sceptical about any government's claim to be on the side of justice. It was argued in the 1930s, as now, that the issues were so confused, the unrighteousness so evenly distributed, that we cannot choose. One of the issues about which Niebuhr felt most strongly was that despite this we still do have to choose. In the light of the absolute value of love we can and must make discriminate judgements. He was particularly scathing about those Americans who were hesitant to come into the Second World War because of the record of imperialism by the Allies.

Despite the apparent relativity of every conflict there are certain issues in which we can and must choose the lesser evil. This is so in the social struggle where we must choose for the powerless against those who enjoy inordinate privilege: but it is also true in the international sphere. The alternative is total relativity.

> If it is not possible to express a moral preference for the justice achieved in democratic societies, in comparison with tyrannical societies, no historical preference has any meaning.[24]

Which is the lesser of the two evils, however? Yoder accused Niebuhr of having a sentimental depreciation of the horrors of war.[25] Even *a priori* it is unlikely that a man of his generation would be unaware of the horrors of World War One. In fact the entries in *Leaves from the Notebook of a Tamed Cynic*, his chairmanship, for a time, of the Fellowship of Reconciliation and other explicit statements belie this.[26] Niebuhr, on the other hand, accused pacifists of always preferring tyranny to resistance. The horror of modern war is such that even without nuclear weapons there is a *prima facie* case for pacifism. Indeed, the modern debate between the Pacifist and the Niebuhrian can legitimately begin with the assumption that war must be ruled out as the greatest conceivable evil. The burden of proof is on the non-pacifist to show that there is an even greater evil than modern war. The pacifist can point to the ability of occupied nations to keep their culture and values intact, to the inevitability of change, to the resources of love and prayer and to the hope that God will eventually bring release to the captive. The realist will be against these two rather bleak considerations. First, will any group that has achieved absolute power willingly give it up? What examples can be pointed to? People relinquish power when they are forced to do so and it is a strange assumption that bloody civil war is less horrific than other kinds of conflict. Secondly, what kind of tyranny is it? All societies have been characterized by spasmodic oppression, cruelty, corruption and injustice. This is very different from long standing tyrannies in the grip of an ideology that reinforces absolute control. In George Orwell's *1984* Winston Smith and his girl-friend believe they can defeat the society around them. Although they know they will be caught and killed they think they can win by dying hating the system. The pathos of the novel is that as a result of ruthless brainwashing they die loving big brother. We would have to say that such a society, if it ever came into being, would be the worst evil we could imagine because the possibility of being human no longer existed. This is not to assume that any society now or in the future would become like that, but *1984* acts as a salutary warning. It also questions the assumption that war, however terrible, is the worst evil we can conceive. There may be something to defend which is not simply material well-being, or a way of life, or particular cultural values, but the very possibility of being human.

The horror of modern war cannot be underestimated. Nevertheless, against this we have to set the following considerations. First, most pacifists accept the need to achieve some kind of rough and ready justice, if necessary with the use of minimal coercion, within the state. Is it anything but arbitrary to draw a line between the state and the states-system? Is the international scene to be dominated by those who are prepared to use power in the most ruthless and unprincipled way?

Secondly, we accept the necessity of law within the state. Is the international order to be handed over to total disorder, to complete lawlessness? For the UN being at present so weak, that is what the refusal to resist involves.

Our attempts to achieve justice and to impose law on the international scene are flawed: but so they are within the state. The attempt to procure justice always reflects class or group interest. Nevertheless, we do not abolish the police because they are more likely to protect the interests of the property owners than the dispossessed. More positively, and theologically: are we to refuse to co-operate with God in his work of creating *pax-ordo-iustitia*, that ordered and just peace without which there can be no human life?

Niebuhr believed that pacifism had a legitimate place within the church: that it helped to symbolize and keep alive the perfectionist strand within Christianity. If everyone took the vow of celibacy life would cease. But the vows made by religious witness to a life lived for God alone and similarly with the vows of poverty and obedience.

Few pacifists are content to see their stance in purely vocational terms, something for them but not for others. They are conscious of claims laid on all Christians and potentially on all men as part of their response to, and new life in, Christ. There may here be an irreconcilable difference. For I have argued that we have to live with the tension between this age and the life of the age to come and that so long as God wills earthly life to continue he asks us to co-operate with him in upholding both civil and international order. Consistent pacifism means withdrawal from key areas of public life. There are real differences in assessing the place of pacifism within the Church, yet perhaps this also is part of the tension we are meant to feel. For it is the legitimate desire of the pacifist to universalize the moral claims he experiences that troubles the non-pacifist, and rightly troubles him, for it brings to bear that absolute standard in the light of which our compromises are seen for what they are and to which we are called to conform so far as we can under the conditions of sinful finite existence.

NOTES

1. *Moral Man and Immoral Society*, p. 205.
2. *Moral Man and Immoral Society*, p. 252.
3. *Moral Man and Immoral Society*, p. 254.
4. *Christianity and Power Politics*, p. 10.
5. *Moral Man and Immoral Society*, p. 172.
6. *Christianity and Power Politics*, p. 10.
7. He also maintained with Kant that 'only good will is intrinsically good' *Moral Man and Immoral Society*, p. 173.
8. Ronald Sider and Richard Taylor, *Nuclear Holocaust and Christian Hope*, Hodder and Stoughton, 1983, p. 128 and note 60 on page 389. See also my 'Power, Coercion and Love' in *The Cross and the Bomb*, ed. Francis Bridger, Mowbray, 1983.
9. John 18. 19–24.
10. *Nuclear Holocaust and Christian Hope*, p. 130.
11. Willard Swartley and Alan Kreider in 'Pacifist Christianity: The Kingdom Way', *When Christians Disagree: Pacifism and War*, ed. IVP 1984, argue along the same lines as Sider and Taylor. They allow the legitimacy of coercion – up to a point. The point at which they draw the line is 'permanent physical harm'. But in resisting a violent criminal there will always be the risk that this will occur.
12. James Childress in 'Reinhold Niebuhr's realistic critique of pacifism', an essay in his *Moral Responsibility in Conflict*, Louisiana State University Press, 1982, argues that there is much more significance than Niebuhr allows between direct force and indirect coercion. This is true but it is not in itself enough to justify pacifism. Childress, following Tolstoy says that if a child is about to be attacked: (a) We do not know for certain

that the child will be harmed, and (b) We are not in a position to say that the life of the child is more valuable than that of the attacker. But, on the contrary, we may very well be in a position to know that the child will be harmed. Further, the attacker, in trying to harm the child forfeits his own right to protection. Finally, Christian love leads us to do all we can to save the child from hurt and this outweighs the risk we take that we might seriously harm the attacker.

13. G.H.C. Macgregor, *The Relevance of the Impossible*, The Fellowship of Reconciliation, 1941. A shortened version of the argument is contained in the same author's *The New Testament Basis of Pacifism*, Fellowship of Reconciliation, New and Revised Edition, 1953, pp. 99–105.
14. *Christianity and Power Politics*, p. 2.
15. *The Relevance of the Impossible*, chap 3; *Nuclear Holocaust and Christian Hope*, pp. 179–181; John Yoder, 'Reinhold Niebuhr and Christian Pacifism' in *Mennonite Quarterly Reviews*, April 1955, vol 29, pp. 101–117.
16. John Yoder, *Nevertheless*, Herald Press, 1971, pp. 123–28.
17. John Yoder, *Nevertheless*, Herald Press, 1971, pp. 126–27.
18. *Nuclear Holocaust and Christian Hope*, p. 26.
19. *An Interpretation of Christian Ethics*, p. 67.
20. *Christianity and Power Politics*, p. 11.
21. *The New Testament Basis of Pacifism*, p. 102.
22. *The New Testament Basis of Pacifism*, p. 104.
23. *Nuclear Holocaust and Christian Hope*, p. 322.
24. *Christianity and Power Politics*, p. 28.
25. 'Reinhold Niebuhr and Christian Pacifism', p. 112.
26. *Leaves from the Notebooks of a Tamed Cynic*, p. 68. *Christianity and Power Politics*, p. 31.

Niebuhr's Realistic-Pragmatic Approach to War and 'the Nuclear Dilemma'

JAMES F. CHILDRESS

Introduction

It is impossible to determine which positions Reinhold Niebuhr would have taken in current debates about nuclear deterrence. His judgements in social ethics were often very specific and practical, and they may have expressed his 'moral intuition' or 'moral genius' rather than his ethical perspective and framework. Some observers found his 'critical analysis' more 'brilliant' than his constructive proposals.[1] Niebuhr's thought was marked by various shifts and turns, dictated largely by historical circumstances, developed dialectically, and designed to correct such distortions as 'idealism'. His ethical perspective and framework, often characterized as 'realistic' and 'pragmatic', are still invoked in debates about nuclear policies, but 'realists' are often opponents in these debates, as the names of John Bennett, George Kennan, Kenneth Thompson, William V. O'Brien, and Ernest Lefever suggest.[2] Thus, it may be useful to explore Niebuhr's realistic perspective and pragmatic framework and sketch their implications for war and what he called 'the nuclear dilemma'.

Realistic-Pragmatic Social Ethics

The term 'realism' aptly characterizes Niebuhr's ethical perspective from 1932, when *Moral Man and Immoral Society* appeared, to the end of his life in 1971. He defined 'realism' in moral and social theory as 'the disposition to take all factors in a social and political situation, which offer resistance to established norms, into account, particularly the factors of self-interest and power'.[3] The pursuit of *self-interest* is inevitable, as an expression of 'original sin', and it is magnified in group activity, particularly states. Even though Niebuhr moved away from the sharp dichotomy implied by the title, *Moral Man and Immoral Society*, he still emphasized that individuals and groups have different possibilities of moral transcendence and conceded that his position could be accurately described as 'The Not So Moral Man in His Less Moral Communities'.[4] In a formulation he later rejected as too quantitative, Niebuhr distinguished between 'the equality of sin and the inequality of guilt'.[5] Whatever language is used, his claim is that recognition of the universality and equality of sin does not eradicate moral distinctions within history, for example, between nations in conflict. Even though sin is inevitable, within history there are degrees of moral blameworthiness as well as 'indeterminate possibilities for good and for evil'.

Power can be viewed as the means to realize interests, and it takes many different forms, including military force, the *ultima ratio* of states. Because of the universality of self-interest, there is also a universal drive for power. However, power is also necessary to realize other values, including justice. Moral suasion is important but not sufficient, and coercion is a necessary feature of social life.

Defending 'Christian realism' Niebuhr rejected Hans Morgenthau's claim that 'it is impossible . . . to be a successful politician and a good Christian'. Morgenthau appeared to interpret the moral dilemma of politics as a conflict between morality, on the one hand, and politics, on the other. Niebuhr, by contrast, defined the 'moral ambiguity of the political realm in terms which do not rob it of moral content.'[6] The moral dilemma is not between morality and politics, but within politics. Although Niebuhr recognized perfectionist tendencies in Jesus' statements about non-resistance, he did not suppose that these statements exhaust the moral content and significance of either the New Testament or Scripture as a whole. Other scriptural resources for a realistic perspective in social ethics include: (1) a sense of divine providence – a meaning of history greater than particular schemes of meaning; (2) a doctrine of human nature that recognizes the 'dignity' of humanity as created in God's image but also its 'misery' as sinful; and (3) 'the passion for justice as an expression of the love commandment'.[7]

Niebuhr's realism included both what is normal (self-interest and power) and what is normative ('established norms'), but, because of his battles against pacifists and other idealists, he tended to emphasize how the former resists the latter. Late in his career he worried that his realism had become 'excessively consistent' and had obscured 'the residual capacity for justice and devotion to the larger good' even in collective life.[8] Nevertheless, he insisted that social ethics cannot only consider 'ultimate' norms (e.g., utopian thought about the perfect society) but must also consider 'proximate' norms since it must 'come to terms with the problem of establishing *tolerable harmonies* of life on all levels of *community* under conditions set by the fact that men are sinners.'[9]

While 'realism' characterizes Niebuhr's ethical perspective, 'pragmatism' characterizes his ethical framework, that is, how he attempted to answer questions about what ought to be done: 'When viewing a historic situation all moralists become pragmatists and utilitarians.'[10] Norms are important – to prevent 'realism' from becoming 'cynicism' and 'pragmatism' from becoming 'mere opportunism'. 'Christian pragmatism' – a phrase Niebuhr attributed to Dr Visser t'Hooft – avoids opportunism 'by certain definite principles, upon which, as upon a loom, the fabric of pragmatic decisions is woven'. These principles have to do with the relation of order to justice and with the relation of freedom and equality in the determination of justice.[11]

The principle of *order* – often used interchangeably with *peace* – is derived from an anthropology that emphasizes human sinfulness and organic processes in history under God's providence. The principle of *justice*, defined as rendering to each person or group what is due, itself involves two transcendent norms – *liberty* and *equality* – that cannot simply be realized without conflict and compromise. Determining what is due individuals and groups presupposes balancing liberty and equality, since either principle would destroy society if applied absolutely. The norm of liberty derives from the essential freedom of human beings as spiritual personalities (the *imago dei*), while the norm of equality derives from the transcendent norm of love: equality is 'the best nexus between love and justice, once the calculation of interests and rights must be undertaken'.[12]

All of these principles – order (peace), liberty, and equality, along with love (*agape*) – are universal and are accessible to all human beings, but they are clarified by revelation. They are all transcendent or regulative principles rather than simple possibilities. They *illuminate* but do not *prescribe* what ought to be done. They cannot solve our dilemma because there are no second-order principles to indicate how far one substantive principle should be sacrificed for another in historical circumstances. There are 'no principles which could guide us in choosing between various emphases or various competing or complementary principles, according to the weight they are given by historical contingencies'.[13] For example, in the nuclear dilemma, 'we can sacrifice neither order nor justice.'[14] In the absence of second-order principles Niebuhr's ethical framework depends on dialectical reflection. Indeed, all of these substantive principles are dialectically related: Love and justice; justice and order; liberty and equality. Justice contradicts but also approximates love under conditions of history; or love negates but also fulfils justice. Without some love justice would degenerate into a mere balance of power. The principles of justice are often in tension with the requirements of order, and yet they cannot be realized without order, including such means as coercion to maintain order. But without justice order cannot endure. Within conceptions of justice there is tension between liberty and equality, and it is necessary to compromise one for the sake of the other.[15] The most that can be expected is 'relative peace and relative justice'.[16]

Niebuhr's pragmatic ethical framework clearly focuses on the ends and consequences of actions and policies; it seeks to determine which actions and policies will effectively and efficiently produce a net balance of good over evil. It requires what might be called judgements of proportionality, and it involves 'rational calculation'.[17] Niebuhr did not concentrate on rules, which state that actions of a certain kind ought (or ought not) to be performed because they are right (or wrong), but rather on principles, which identify various ends and consequences of actions as morally relevant. Actions and policies must then be assessed according to their probable consequences, not according to their intrinsic or inherent characteristics. Niebuhr's overall framework is thus consequentialist rather than formalist or deontological. It might be best described as 'pragmatic-consequentialist'. Joining a pragmatic-consequentialist framework with a realistic perspective, Niebuhr emphasized that it is necessary to recognize the limits on the realization of the norms of love, justice, and order because of the persistence of self-interest and the necessity of power, especially coercion. It is frequently necessary to act in morally ambiguous circumstances, to choose the lesser of two evils, and even to incur guilt, recognizing that we are justified by faith and thus freed to be responsible and to do what is necessary.

Resistance, Violence, and War

Modes of resistance, non-violent and violent, have been controversial for Christians and others, who have drawn different lines and set different limits in individual and social responses to evil and injustice:

(i)	(ii)	(iii)	(iv)	(v)
Non-resistance	Non-violent/ Resistance	Limited Violent/ Resistance (Discrimination)	Limited Violent/ Resistance (Proportionality)	Unlimited Violent Resistance

According to Niebuhr, non-resistance as demanded by Jesus is impossible and irresponsible as a political option. The line between non-resistance (i) and other modes of resistance (ii–v) is the critical one; when the decision is made to resist evil and injustice, the remaining choices are largely pragmatic and utilitarian – they are questions of effectiveness and efficiency in producing good consequences, outcomes, and states of affairs. Thus, Niebuhr rejected the absolute distinction between non-violence and violence:

> The religious radical is wrong in believing that there is an intrinsic difference between violence and non-violence. The differences are pragmatic rather than intrinsic. The social consequences of the two methods are different, but the differences are in degree rather than in kind. Both place restraint upon liberty and both may destroy life and property. Once

the principle of coercion and resistance has been accepted as necessary to the social struggle and to social cohesion, and pure pacifism has thus been abandoned, the differences between violence and non-violence lose their absolute significance, though they remain important.[18]

For all modes of resistance, non-violent or violent, the moral questions are the same; they all concern the consequences of the actions, particularly their impact on justice and order.

Niebuhr also rejected the fifth position on the spectrum because it focuses on only one end – the eradication of evil or injustice – without any regard for other consequences, such as the destruction of human life or the order that can be achieved after conflict. In its own way it is as alien to an acceptable social ethic as the first position, which at least reflects the demands of the New Testament, however impracticable they may be. The fifth position is often expressed in the language of a 'righteous' or 'holy' war against the forces of evil and injustice. Despite the obvious temptation to view the war against Hitler as a 'holy war', Niebuhr insisted on distinguishing the 'proximate goals of justice' expressed in the war from the holiness represented by God. The cause was not 'holy' in the sense of being 'unqualifiedly good', the achievements of its defenders were 'ambiguous', particularly since they had contributed to the rise of Hitler, and the weapons were 'terrible' rather than holy. Nevertheless, it is essential to make discriminating judgements while recognizing the universal taint of sin:

It is not possible to achieve this pure holiness; and yet we must act. The Christian acts with an uneasy conscience both because of the ambiguity of his cause and the impurity of his weapons. His conscience can be easy only as he is 'justified by faith', and not by the achievement of holiness or by what is worse, the pretension of holiness.[19]

Eschewing the false alternatives of (i) and (v), the alternatives of religious inaction and religious fanaticism, Niebuhr located the serious debate among (ii), (iii), and (iv). The fundamental evils in actions to resist evil and injustice are self-interest and coercive power. However, there are different mixes of self-regard and other-regard, and modes of coercive resistance can be distinguished according to their consequences.

It is important to note that the first four positions on the above spectrum *disavow* some means of resistance and that their arguments for adhering to those limits are fundamentally the same. Their basic theological-ethical argument is that human beings are not responsible for every evil or injustice that happens if the only effective means of resistance would cross the line or transgress the limit set on resistance; finally, they are not responsible for making history come out right, since God is in control of history.[20] Subsidiary arguments focus on the limited human capacity to predict, produce, and assess outcomes. By contrast the fifth position identifies human resistance to evil with God's eradication of evil.

The terms 'disavow' and 'disavowal' appear throughout Niebuhr's discussions of limits of resistance, and he insisted that it is not morally acceptable to 'disavow' any means of resistance in principle. Disavowal can occur only in particular situations, according to the prediction and assessment of consequences. Yet earlier Niebuhr had been a pacifist. He defined 'pacifism' as expressing one's 'critical attitude toward the use of force by *disavowing* it completely in at least one important situation', and he disavowed the use of force in international conflicts. His pacifism was pragmatic in a negative sense; he contended that international violence would be 'worthless' and 'suicidal'.[21] In the late nineteen-thirties he surrendered the last vestiges of his pacifism, claiming that 'it is not possible to disavow war absolutely without disavowing the task of establishing justice'.[22]

Niebuhr's realistic anthropology and his realistic sociology (e.g. society is a 'perpetual state of war') imply that the institution of war is inevitable as an expression of self-interest and the will to power; they do not, however, justify any particular wars. Because we are already and always engaged in 'war', undertaking a particular war may not appear to be such a large step, but moral justification is required and even inevitable. Even though Niebuhr viewed the distinction between non-violence and violence as only a matter of degree, he nevertheless viewed international violence or war as the *ultima ratio*, the last resort. It may not be wholly consistent to reduce the distinction between non-violence and violence as far as he did and yet to claim that war is the *ultima ratio*, but Niebuhr held that the differences in degrees of consequences are sufficient to require that war be the last resort.[23]

Even though their motives are always mixed and ambiguous, nations engage in the process of moral justification. Niebuhr doubted that any nation in history has ever been able to say 'This war may not be moral, but in our own self-interest we have to fight it anyway'. Agreeing with Hans Morgenthau that the 'moral reasons given by nations for their actions are pretences to justify their national self-interests', Niebuhr did not dismiss these justifications as mere rationalizations, ideologies, or bad faith. Rather, he insisted, 'people, even nations, engage in this pretense because they are moral'.[24] This is consistent with his affirmation of La Rochefoucauld's maxim: hypocrisy is the tribute that vice pays to virtue. Unmasking hypocrisy, as Niebuhr recognized, is one important mode of moral criticism.

Because of the essential (but limited) moral nature of human beings, nations have to justify their departures from peace (order), and they do so in the name of justice and peace. Over many centuries in the west these justifications of departures from peace (order) have been systematized and structured – especially but not only in the Roman Catholic context – in just-war theories that offer criteria for the justification and limitation of particular wars and their conduct. The following criteria, with some variations, appear in most comprehensive just-war theories: legitimate or competent authority; just cause; right intention; announcement of intention (often called declaration of war); last resort; reasonable hope of success; proportionality; and just conduct. All of these criteria, except for the last one, establish the *jus ad bellum*, the right to go to war, while the last criterion focuses on the *jus in bello*, right conduct within war, which includes both right intention and proportionality, as well as some other standards.[25]

As James Johnson has noted, Niebuhr did not so much 'rediscover' as 'reinvent' just-war theory.[26] This process of reinvention was shaped in part by his opponents, the pacifists, and he thus tended to concentrate on the *jus ad bellum*, the right to go to war, rather than the *jus in bello*. Within both, his reasoning was primarily pragmatic and consequentialist; it reflected the principle of proportionality rather than intrinsic limits on the conduct of war. Several times Niebuhr objected to the elaborate, rigid, inflexible, artificial, and absolute formulations of traditional just-war theories, contending that they were 'more likely to confuse than to illumine the conscience.'[27] He preferred a simpler, more flexible approach in accord with his pragmatic framework, even though it offered less precise guidance. Even as he became more sympathetic to Roman Catholic moral theology later in his life, and as several Protestants, particularly Paul Ramsey, began to appropriate the tradition of just war, there is no evidence that Niebuhr significantly modified his criticisms, some of which fail to appreciate the tradition's flexibility in the interpretation of absolute standards.[28]

Niebuhr still invoked some criteria of traditional just-war theories in the process of criticizing or explicitly rejecting them, and they played a role in his justification of World War Two and the Korean War and in his opposition to the War in Vietnam.[29] He usually presupposed rather than explicitly discussed the first criterion, *legitimate authority*, but he emphasized the second criterion: a (relatively) *just cause* is indispensable for a just-war. As I have already noted, he also invoked the criterion of *last resort*, the exhaustion of other alternatives. This criterion does not necessarily reduce just wars to the distinction between aggressor/ defender or condemn the side that first resorts to armed force. Although *announcement of intention* is often interpreted legalistically as a formal declaration of war, it can be connected with the requirement to explain and justify the departure from peace (order) as well as the requirement that war be the last resort since ultimata or formal declarations of war 'are the last measures of persuasion short of force itself'.[30]

The criteria of *reasonable chance of success* and *proportionality* are closely connected, and Niebuhr criticized both of them, even though it can be argued that both are at least implicit in his justification and limitation of war. He noted that Churchill fortunately defied the criterion of 'fair chance of success'.[31] But he failed to appreciate the flexibility of the application of this criterion in the tradition, and its total rejection is incompatible with his pragmatic-consequentialist framework. There is room for vigorous debate about

what constitutes a 'reasonable' or 'fair' chance of success, but if a war has no reasonable chance of success,
it is imprudent, and if a nation can realize none of the
ends that allegedly justify the war, then it should certainly reconsider whether the war is justified. Furthermore, the just-war tradition has applied this criterion
more clearly to offensive than to defensive wars, and
'success' is not limited to 'victory', as Niebuhr emphasized in his analysis of resistance in the nuclear age.[32]
It may even include *witness* to such important values
as justice when resistance is not likely to be an effective *instrument* to realize them. At the very least, it
precludes totally useless and pointless warfare. This
criterion is more acceptable within and perhaps even
required by a pragmatic-consequentialist framework
than Niebuhr supposed.

The criteria of proportionality and right intention
are important bridges between the *jus ad bellum* and
the *jus in bello* since they function in both areas.
Although Niebuhr's pragmatic framework for war con-
sisted primarily of the principle of proportionality, he
objected to the use of this criterion in Roman Catholic
theories of just war, but his objection is ambiguous.
He affirmed the 'good idea' of the traditional doctrine
of proportionality between means and ends of action,
but he insisted that it has 'no light for the present
generation' and that it is 'false now' because of
nuclear weapons.[33] In fact, his interpretation of the
'nuclear dilemma' is set by the principle of proportionality: we cannot use nuclear weapons without 'destroying the moral fabric of our nation' and yet they
cannot be 'simply disavowed without courting surrender'.[34] It is probably more accurate to interpret Niebuhr as holding that the criterion of proportionality
offers no easy or final answer to the problems of war
and nuclear deterrence, rather than as rejecting it altogether. Whatever his language, his moral assessment of

wars and their conduct hinged on the principle of
proportionality – the requirement to produce the best
possible balance of good over bad consequences. This
principle excludes excessive violence and unnecessary
suffering, since both 'excessive' and 'unnecessary' are
determined in part by the ends and probable consequences of actions.

The criterion of right intention, which is important
for the conduct of war as well as for the war as a
whole, obviously includes the intention of justice,
already reflected in the requirement of a just cause. In
addition, right intention excludes such motives as
hatred and vindictiveness. Although it is important to
distinguish motives and actions, a total separation is
impossible, and Niebuhr frequently criticized hatred
and vindictiveness, partly because of their consequences and partly because of their incompatibility with
love. According to Niebuhr, agents have greater possibilities of moral transcendence in motives and attitudes than in actions, and he claimed that 'in so far as
it is possible to defend a cause, not primarily because
it is to our interest to do so, but because we regard
the cause as objectively right, it is also possible to
contend against the opponents of that cause without
hatred'.[35] 'Non-hatred is a much more important sign
and symbol of Christian faith than non-violence.'[36]
Nevertheless, it would be unrealistic to overlook the
process of dehumanization of the enemy that occurs
in the preparation for and the conduct of war.[37]

Finally, right intention also includes peace (order)
as the object or end of war; this is usually combined
with the intention of justice under the rubric of a 'just
peace'. There is legitimate concern that emphasis on
peace as the object or end of war may justify doing
everything possible to bring the war to a quick conclusion. Nevertheless, if one also emphasizes that peace
(order) cannot endure without justice, then conduct

in and after the war becomes very important. For example, Niebuhr recognized the moral imperative to avoid 'such destruction as would undermine the basis for future peace'.[38]

Some implications of the criteria of right intention and proportionality have already been sketched for the conduct of war, since they apply to both the *jus ad bellum* and the *jus in bello*. For purposes of simplification, we can distinguish between modes of resistance (iii) and (iv) according to whether they limit violence by the principle of discrimination – non-combatant immunity from direct attack – or only by the principle of proportionality. The traditional Roman Catholic position has accepted proportionate judgements about indirect deaths of non-combatants, but not about direct deaths of non-combatants, the latter being ruled out as immoral. Niebuhr, however, explicitly considered only proportionality and refused to disavow any means as intrinsically wrong and absolutely forbidden, even though he criticized obliteration bombing as 'indiscriminate'.[39] Viewing the bombing of cities as 'a vivid revelation of the whole moral ambiguity of warfare', Niebuhr held in the summer of 1943 that:

> It is not possible to defeat a foe without causing innocent people to suffer with the guilty. It is not possible to engage in any act of collective opposition to collective evil without involving the innocent with the guilty. It is not possible to move in history without becoming tainted with guilt. Once bombing has been developed as an instrument of warfare, it is not possible to *disavow* its use without capitulating to the foe who refuses to *disavow* it.[40]

He viewed the bombing policies as 'tragic necessities', emphasizing that 'no man has the moral freedom to escape from these hard and cruel necessities of history'. It is possible, however, to gain moral transcendence in the attitudes taken toward necessities, particularly to avoid 'rancour or self-righteousness'. Praising the consciences of the pilots of bombing planes who refused to take Communion before their trips, Niebuhr noted that the Lord's Supper mediates God's mercy 'not only to those who repent of the sins they have done perversely but also to those who repent of the sins in which they are involved inexorably by reason of their service to a "just cause" '.[41] Later he held that 'it would be hazardous to draw absolute distinctions between what is, and what is not, permissible in total war'. The 'melancholy necessities of total war' are the consequences of a technical society that 'makes the harnessing of the total resources of a society for the destruction of the foe possible and therefore necessary'. According to Niebuhr, 'the necessity follows from the possibility, because once the instruments of a total war are unloosed they will guarantee defeat for the side that *fails to use* them, whether from want of resolution, or failure of organization, or moral scruple.'[42]

In 1944 Niebuhr denied that Allied 'area' or 'obliteration' bombing was justified by military necessity. It is useful to contrast Niebuhr's brief article 'Is the Bombing Necessary?' with 'The Morality of Obliteration Bombing' by John C. Ford, S.J. in the same year.[43] Ford focused on 'the natural-law rights of non-combatants' that are violated by obliteration bombing and contended that 'it is impossible to adopt this strategy without having the direct intent of violating the rights of innocent civilians. This intent is, of course, gravely immoral.' But even if this intent had not been present and the destruction had been indirect, it would still have been wrong because it lacked a proportionately grave cause. By contrast, Niebuhr started with the question of necessity. Rejecting a sharp dichotomy between 'human values' and 'military necessity' and refusing to make the latter merely a matter of military expertise, he argued that the shift from a policy of precision bombing to 'indiscriminate bombing of whole areas' had never been explained or justified by the government and that conceivable justifications were not cogent – for example, that 'the bombing of workers' homes represents an indirect destruction of industrial power' or a reprisal for Rotterdam and Warsaw. As long as there were other alternatives, the actions of physical destruction were not warranted and were even counter-productive. Obliteration bombing stemmed in part from a negative conception of the war aim – defeating Hitler – and a policy of unconditional surrender. Nevertheless, in contrast to Ford, Niebuhr was willing to assess the indiscriminate means according to their probable consequences. While Niebuhr would hold that the ends (including probable consequences) justify the means, a defender of position (iii), such as Ford or Paul Ramsey, would hold that the ends (including probable consequences) justify the means, but only means that pass an independent moral inspection or audit.[44]

Since Niebuhr refused to rule out any means absolutely and unconditionally and appealed only to the principle of proportionality, his approach is similar, at first glance, to act utilitarians who hold that agents should choose the course of action that would probably maximise universal (not egoistic) welfare. The rules of war are mere maxims or rules of thumb that can be disregarded or set aside without moral qualms and guilt, because they only summarize previous human experience about the effects of actions. This position can be found in Joseph Fletcher's *Situation Ethics*, which considers the decision to drop the atomic bomb as an 'agapeic calculus'.[45] In the final analysis, Niebuhr's position is more complex because he suggests – perhaps not wholly consistently – that such violations of the rules of war as indiscriminate bombing are justified only by necessity, involve guilt, and should be occasions for repentance.

Niebuhr's approach is thus close to what Michael Walzer calls 'utilitarianism of extremity'. Its motto is 'do justice unless the heavens are (really) about to fall', and its key words are emergency and necessity. Walzer does not appeal lightly to necessity, nor did Niebuhr, for the nature, imminence, and avoidability of the danger are of primary importance. Hence utilitarianism of extremity is not reducible to ordinary calculations of consequences, such as the number of lives that will probably be saved or lost by a particular military action. It requires extraordinary circumstances. For example, British terror bombing of German cities, Walzer argues, was probably justified early in World War Two when the outcome of the war was in doubt and there was a danger 'of an unusual and horrifying kind'. Nazism was 'an ultimate threat to everything decent in our lives' and the consequences of its final victory 'were literally beyond calculation, immeasurably awful'.[45] What Niebuhr argued with reference to the *jus ad bellum* would also apply to the *jus in bello*: 'The question whether or not we should declare war [against Hitler] is therefore not primarily one of morals but of strategy in the sense that I believe we ought to do *whatever has to be done* to prevent the triumph of this intolerable tyranny.'[47]

In supreme emergencies, Walzer argues, the rules of war still have force, and the agents who violate them have 'dirty hands'.[48] Hence we may feel compelled to say both 'right' and 'wrong' about the same acts and perhaps refuse to honour agents who have 'dirty hands' in situations of necessity because of the 'moral traces' or 'residual effects' of the rules of war.[49]

Walzer sharply distinguishes his position from the 'realists', but he ignores important differences among the realists – for example, between Reinhold Niebuhr and Hans Morgenthau. Indeed, Niebuhr's perspective is very close to Walzer's own perspective on moral necessity and guilt.[50] A major difference between Niebuhr and Walzer is Niebuhr's appeal to the doctrine of justification by faith to overcome the moral paralysis that might result from an emphasis on moral ambiguity, guilt, and tragedy. Another major difference is Niebuhr's lack of clarity about several matters, particularly about how our moral judgements are pragmatic and consequentialist and yet we are guilty (and should feel guilty) about violating the rules of war under conditions of necessity. On the one hand, Niebuhr's general theoretical position does not appear to assign weight to moral rules, apart from the consequences of actions. On the other hand, the language of ambiguity, lesser of two evils, and guilt often suggests that these rules are independent of the consequences of actions, sometimes being over-ridden by, but sometimes over-riding, appeals to the consequences. The function of the rules of war in Niebuhr's thought is often analogous to the theological use of the law: these rules drive us to repentance, but they do not restrain us (civil use of the law) if the consequences of adherence would be terrible.

Two dangers of the appeal to necessity should be noted. First, 'necessity' often becomes a cloak for mere military utility, further undermining rules of war, as happened in World War Two. Second, the language of necessity may lead agents to believe that they have no choice when in fact they do. Even if some actions are the only means to some ends, the ends themselves may be subject to criticism. If the ends are not necessary, then the means to those ends are not necessary. Perhaps in some cases a nation should surrender its independence and its territory if it cannot preserve them without violating the principle of discrimination. There may be moral limits to national survival and the pursuit of other moral values. Niebuhr recognized such moral limits, but they were set by the principle of proportionality, not by the deontological principle of discrimination.

Nuclear Weapons, Conflicts, and Deterrence

It is important to put Niebuhr's discussion of nuclear weapons, conflicts, and deterrence or what he called 'the nuclear dilemma' in the context of his realistic perspective, his pragmatic framework, and their application to war in general, because he did not recognize an intrinsic moral distinction between non-nuclear and nuclear weapons. He approached weapons as he approached other means of securing tolerable justice and peace in the world; all actions are to be evaluated according to their probable consequences. The judgement that nuclear weapons are not evil *per se* is required by his ethical framework.

It has been suggested, by Hans Morgenthau, among others, that Niebuhr justified the use of the atomic bomb against Hiroshima and Nagasaki,[51] but there is clear evidence that he had serious moral reservations about it. He recognized that thte atomic bomb's development could not be avoided in the struggle with Germany, and he admitted that its use may have been determined by 'historic forces more powerful than any human decision'. But in the fall of 1945 he criticized statesmen for their lack of imagination in developing ways to gain the benefits of the weapon's availability without its indiscriminate destruction: 'we reached the level of Nazi morality in justifying the use of the bomb on the ground that it shortened the war.'[52] Its use was not a matter of necessity. Niebuhr also signed the Calhoun report that denounced the bomb's 'morally indefensible' and 'irresponsible use' and stressed the importance of 'contrition' and 'penitence'.[53]

With the development of nuclear weapons by the USSR and other countries, the world faces what Niebuhr called 'the nuclear dilemma'. In accord with his overall ethical framework, Niebuhr emphasized in 1961, 'I know of no general principle, Christian or otherwise, which will solve the cold war and the nuclear dilemma'.[54] Any Niebuhrian approach to the nuclear dilemma must be realistic and pragmatic, emphasizing the dialectical relation of the principles of peace (order) and justice (liberty and equality) in application to probable consequences of different courses of action.

Niebuhr's use of the phrase 'nuclear dilemma' underlined his conviction that there was no easy or final solution to the problems occasioned by the development and spread of nuclear weapons. He rejected as unchristian the view that life is tragic, holding that it is more ironic than tragic because 'destructiveness is not an inevitable consequence of human creativity'. Nevertheless, 'there are, of course, tragic moments and tragic choices in life. There are situations in which a choice must be made between equally valid loyalties and one value must be sacrificed to another.' His major examples of this sort of tragedy were the conflict between Antigone and Creon and modern deterrence: 'We have already observed the tragic character of the dilemma which modern democratic nations face, when forced to risk atomic warfare in order to avoid the outbreak of war. The alternatives to this dilemma, proposed by moralists and idealists of various types, will prove upon close scrutiny to involve a dubious sacrifice of some cherished value; in this instance the security of our civilization.'[55]

The term 'dilemma' suggests that there are good reasons for and against an act or policy; a dilemma is 'moral' when the reasons in conflict are moral rather than political, legal, economic, etc. Niebuhr was not very precise in his use of the term 'dilemma', but his characterization of the 'nuclear dilemma' as 'tragic' suggests a situation in which no available action can avoid the sacrifice or risk of some important values: 'the dread nuclear weapons cannot be used without destroying the moral fabric of the nation', and yet 'they cannot be simply disavowed without courting surrender'.[56]

It has been suggested that Niebuhr became a 'nuclear pacifist'.[57] In applying just-war criteria, particularly proportionality and discrimination, to nuclear weapons, nuclear pacifists may *disavow* (a) possession, (b) use, (c) first use, (d) priority of nuclear weapons over conventional weapons in defence, (e) any war that might escalate into nuclear conflict, etc. Thus, the label 'nuclear pacifism' is unclear without further specification, and it is important to determine what, if anything, Niebuhr disavowed about nuclear weapons.

Niebuhr's rejection of all-out nuclear war was emphatic: 'nuclear war is certainly out of proportion to any ends'.[58] He emphasized its terrible moral consequences: 'If the bomb were ever used, I would hope it would kill me, because the *moral situation* would be something that I could not contemplate.'[59] This 'moral situation' would include not only horrendous misery, suffering, and death, but also the heavy burden of moral guilt. The use of nuclear weapons would be 'suicidal' in a moral as well as a physical sense. In the debate about the initiation of a nuclear conflict over Berlin, Niebuhr argued that the discussants had neglected the 'moral consequences of initiating the dread conflict' and asked whether 'a civilization loaded with this monstrous guilt [could] have enough moral health to survive'.[60] But it is not clear whether Niebuhr always limited that moral guilt – elsewhere he talked about 'moral annihilation', 'moral destruction', and 'moral degradation' – to the *initiation* of a nuclear war or also included any *use* of nuclear weapons, even in retaliation. In any event, his view about moral guilt focused on the consequences of the use of nuclear weapons rather than on the violation of the principle of discrimination between combatants and non-combatants.

Yet Niebuhr did not recommend disavowal of the *possession* of nuclear weapons as some nuclear pacifists, defending nuclear realism, have urged.[61] Disavowal in the form of unilateral disarmament is unrealistic and irresponsible in the light of the Soviet threat. Even disavowal in the form of an *announced* intention never to use the weapons might also have morally unacceptable consequences: 'you cannot disavow [their] use absolutely prematurely without bowing yourself out of responsibility for the whole generation'.[62]

In general, Niebuhr held that nations do not have the moral freedom or transcendence to disavow the possession or all uses of nuclear weapons. To do so would sacrifice both order (peace) and justice. But other disavowals may be possible and justifiable, and Niebuhr proposed a policy of no-first use of the hydrogen bomb. He recommended its development and argued against pacifists, nuclear or otherwise, who would renounce its use altogether. Nevertheless, nations may have enough moral transcendence to 'make a solemn covenant never to use it [the hydrogen bomb] first'. Such a 'disavowal', Niebuhr argued, could allay apprehension about its use by the US and its allies, could restrain the defence department's undue reliance upon it, and could counteract tendencies to subordinate moral and political power to military power. It could also express the important belief that 'even a nation can reach the point where it can purchase its life too dearly. If we had to use this kind of destruction in order to save our lives, would we find life worth living?'[63] All of these reasons are consequentialist, in accord with Niebuhr's realistic perspective and pragmatic framework. Although Niebuhr's argument was limited to only one weapon in particular historical circumstances, it does indicate that he would not always, on realistic and pragmatic grounds, repudiate a policy of 'no first use', as recently proposed (and opposed) by people with realist credentials. A Niebuhrian would consider the historical situation very carefully, balancing all of the relevant factors, particularly the probable effects of different courses of action on peace (order) and justice.

Some of Niebuhr's arguments could also support a non-public disavowal of the use of nuclear weapons even in second-strike, even though they do not support a public disavowal, which could be predicted to invite aggression. However, in assessing nuclear deterrence Niebuhr spent little time analysing specific intentions, such as the intention to deceive or to commit murder, focusing instead on the way actions compromise or sacrifice values in their consequences. By contrast, several other contemporary approaches concentrate on specific intentions. For example, Paul Ramsey has worried about whether possession of strategic nuclear weapons is equivalent to an intention or conditional willingness to commit murder, concluding at one point that nuclear deterrence is a situation of 'studied ambiguity' with an intention to deceive. The American Catholic Bishops offered their 'conditional acceptance' of nuclear deterrence only after first determining that it did not presuppose the intention or conditional willingness to commit murder: 'it is not morally acceptable to intend to kill the innocent as part of a strategy of deterring nuclear war.' Michael Walzer, however, contends that the system of nuclear deterrence is immoral because it rests ultimately on an immoral threat of murder – directly to kill innocent civilians – but that this immoral murderous threat is morally necessary, at least for the time being.[64] As in the discussion of warfare, Niebuhr's position on deterrence is closer to Walzer's than to Ramsey's or major Catholic statements, but, in contrast to Walzer, Niebuhr devoted little attention to moral rules and specific intentions, concentrating instead on the conflicts between values that structure assessments of probable outcomes.

Within a system of nuclear deterrence, according to Niebuhr, the danger that a conventional conflict will escalate into a nuclear conflict restricts the justification of war. In the mid-nineteen fifties, stressing the relation of the demands of order and justice, Niebuhr (with Angus Dun) held that wars can qualify as just when 'the demands of justice join the demands of order' as in a war to defend the victims of wanton aggression, 'the clearest case'. But when 'the immediate claims of order and justice conflict', as in a war to liberate the oppressed, it is less clear that the war is just. 'The claims of justice are no less. But because contemporary war places so many moral values in incalculable jeopardy, the immediate claims of order have become much greater.' As we have seen, Niebuhr did not recognize any second-order principles to assign priorities to substantive principles in conflict; moral judgement depends on a careful balancing of the principles in actual historical circumstances. Even though peace (order) depends on justice and cannot long endure without justice and even though justice may even be said to have 'the prior claim', the 'nuclear dilemma' gives 'the claims of order [peace] a certain *immediate priority* over the claims of justice'. Within traditional just-war categories, in some situations it would be possible to say that some requirements of the *jus ad bellum* have been met – particularly just cause and perhaps even last resort – but that other requirements have not been met – particularly reasonable chance of success and proportionality. Nevertheless, Niebuhr contended that even in the nuclear age, 'it does not seem possible to draw a line in advance, beyond which it would be better to yield than to resist', and he refused to agree with the technological or nuclear pacifists who contended that 'the excessive violence of atomic warfare has ended the possibility of a just war'.[65] But the possibilities are more limited.

What do Niebuhr's realistic perspective and pragmatic framework imply about *limited* nuclear conflicts? The phrase 'limited nuclear conflict' is ambiguous, since it could include several different limits in contrast to a total, all-out nuclear war. First, it might be waged for *limited goals*. In World War Two Niebuhr criticized the policy of total war that resulted in part from the Allies' war aims, and for any war in the nuclear age it is important to distinguish 'resistance to aggression, designed to deny it victory and tyrannical control' from 'victory by those who resist the aggressor'. 'In view of war's new dimension of annihilation, the justificaiton for a defensive war of limited objectives, to prevent conquest and to force an end to hostilities, does not apply equally to the objectives of bringing an aggressor to unconditional surrender and punishment. Because the ultimate consequences of atomic warfare cannot be measured, only the most imperative demands of justice have a clear sanction.'[66]

A second approach to limited nuclear conflict focuses on the limits recognized by position (iii): moral limits other than proportionality on the means employed, particularly the limits set on legitimate *targets* by the principle of discrimination. Some have argued that a nuclear exchange limited to 'counterforce' rather than 'countervalue' targets could be morally acceptable. Although such an exchange may satisfy the principle of discrimination, it is also necessary to satisfy the principle of proportionality. In the late fifties, Niebuhr considered the possible use of 'tactical' nuclear weapons (approximately the size of the bomb that was dropped on Nagasaki) in contrast to 'strategic' nuclear weapons (the hydrogen bomb), and concluded that even a dozen 'tactical' bombs in Europe or Asia 'would mean the destruction of any moral claim for our civilization'.[67] He based this conclusion on the principle of proportionality. The availability of smaller nuclear warheads, which can be delivered with greater precision, has now shifted the debate about both discrimination and proportionality. Since conventional conflicts could be vastly more indiscriminate, devastating, and destructive than a limited nuclear exchange, the question is whether there is a reasonable chance of limiting the nuclear exchange and thus whether it can be justified by proportionality.[68]

Other approaches to limited nuclear conflict reflect the principle of proportionality and attempt to constrain the destruction relative to limited objectives. These approaches are close to position (iv) on the spectrum, which Niebuhr defended. The limited might include not only the types of nuclear weapons used but also geographical limits (e.g. avoidance of enlargement of the area of nuclear exchange) and temporal limits (e.g. early termination of nuclear conflict). Still another possible limit, closely connected with the others, is reduction of collateral damage to civilians, including harm to future generations. In principle, nuclear conflict could be limited in each of these ways and could be considered morally acceptable.

The critical question about limited nuclear conflict for a realistic-pragmatic approach is whether such a conflict would probably remain limited. Many scenarios of limited nuclear conflict are excessively idealistic since they presuppose measures of rational control and reciprocity that are difficult to imagine in a crisis without historical parallels. As Ian Clark has argued, 'the theorists of limited nuclear war have attempted to create a new code of nuclear chivalry, every bit as colourful and fanciful as the medieval chivalric displays'. This Niebuhrian point can be made in relation to a 'negotiated terminaton of the war after a few limited nuclear exchanges between the parties'. 'It is surely naive', Clarke claims, 'to believe that the mutuality of interests necessary for war-limitation is unattainable before war but to expect it to emerge when the positions of the antagonists are, *a fortiori*, polarized by hostilities.'[69] Critics of Clarke's view contend that 'the impossibility of a limited nuclear war is both historically unproven and by no means logically necessary'.[70] But the question is where the burden of proof rests in view of the major problems of 'command and control' in a limited nuclear exchange. Applying the criterion of 'reasonable hope of success in bringing about justice and peace', the American Catholic Bishops ask 'whether a reasonable hope can exist once nuclear weapons have been exchanged' and insist that 'the burden of proof remains on those who assert that meaningful limitation is possible'.[71] On the basis of his explicit statements, as well as his realistic perspective and pragmatic framework, it is reasonable to suppose that Niebuhr would also put the burden of proof on arguments for crossing the nuclear threshold, firebreak, or boundary because of the significant risks involved. The term 'risk' includes both probability and magnitude of a negative outcome. If there is a low probability that nuclear conflict can be limited and if unlimited nuclear conflict would be disastrous, a realistic-pragmatic approach would disavow a limited nuclear exchange. But such a disavowal can only be made in actual historical circumstances and can never be final and absolute. It depends in part on the psychological signficance of the boundary between conventional and nuclear conflicts since there is no intrinsic moral distinction between conventional and nuclear weapons.

A Niebuhrian realistic perspective and pragmatic framework would recognize that nuclear deterrence is necessary, at least for the foreseeable future. The relative peace (order) of the system of nuclear deterrence – 'the cause of our ultimate insecurity and of our immediate security'[72] – cannot be disregarded, neglected, or immediately dismantled. But acceptance of the 'balance of terror' and its constituent parts is based on the principle of proportionality, not on the principle of discrimination. Deterrence is required because of the international situation. Even though Niebuhr's response to communism became more differentiated and nuanced in the 1960s, he still opposed the totalitarian and expansionist tendencies of the USSR from the standpoint of the principle of justice (particularly the sacrifice of liberty) and peace (order). However, when he viewed 'co-existence' as 'not a good but lesser of two evils',[73] he did not recommend a 'holy' war but emphasized the immediate (though not ultimate) priority of the claims of peace or order over justice in the nuclear age. It is imperative to 'avoid Hell and nuclear disaster'.[74] Just as he repudiated position (i) because of its irresponsibility, he repudiated position (v) because of its identification of ambiguous human opposition to evil with the unambiguous divine will: 'the first duty of Christian faith is to preserve a certain distance between the sanctities of faith and the ambiguities of politics'.[75] Even though Niebuhr emphasized military power as the *ultima ratio* of nations, he just as consistently emphasized that it must be subordinated to other modes of power, and he increasingly stressed the residual capacity for justice and the common good especially in the face of the threat of nuclear disaster.

Deterrence is necessary but not sufficient for both relative peace (order) and relative justice. While it is not morally possible to disavow the possession of nuclear weapons, Niebuhr recognized that nations have enough moral transcendence to disavow 'first use' of strategic weapons. Whether a realistic-pragmatic approach implies a declaratory policy of 'no first use' of tactical nuclear weapons for NATO in the 1980s depends completely on an assessment of complex historical circumstances in the light of probable consequences of alternative courses of action. Indeed, a Niebuhrian would assess all existing and proposed policies, including research, development, and deployment of weapons and negotiations for arms control and reduction, from a realistic perspective and pragmatic framework emphasizing peace (order) and justice. Realists expect to 'confront shifts and turns in foreign policy'.[76] Whether the debate is about a policy of 'no first use', negotiation of strategic arms limitation, deployment of the MX Missile, development of 'Star Wars', priority of offensive or defensive weapons, priority of conventional or nuclear forces, development of 'war-fighting' capability of nuclear forces, or superiority or adequacy of nuclear weapons, a Niebuhrian's response would depend on reading the signs of the times and making judgements of prudence in relation to the values of peace (order) and justice, including the nation's self-interest. For example, realists can be expected to disagree about whether counterforce threats lower the nuclear threshold and make nuclear war more thinkable and likely, or whether countervalue threats are not credible and increase the possibility of war, including nuclear war. Rather than applying the principle of discrimination to the system of nuclear deterrence, the realist-pragmatic approach focuses on the overall ends and consequences. A Niebuhrian would suspect any simplistic approaches to the 'nuclear dilemma', calling attention to their sacrifice of important values, but would hold that we 'may find all sorts of proximate solutions if we have the humility to recognize that the ultimate solution is beyond the competence of mortal men'.[77]*

NOTES

1. Emil Brunner, 'Some Remarks on Reinhold Niebuhr's Work as a Christian Thinker', *Reinhold Niebuhr: His Religious, Social and Political Thought*, 2nd ed., ed. Charles Kegley (New York: Pilgrim Press, 1984), pp. 84–85.
2. See, for example, the chapters by John Bennett and Kenneth Thompson in Kegley, ed., *Reinhold Niebuhr*; George Kennan, *The Nuclear Delusion* (New York: Pantheon Books, 1982); Ernest W. Lefever and E. Stephen Hunt, eds., *The Apocalyptic Premise: Nuclear Arms Debated* (Washington, D.C.: Ethics and Public Policy Center, 1982), which includes 'realistic' selections by Michael Novak and Wolfhart Pannenberg; William V. O'Brien, 'The Challenge of War: A Christian Perspective', *The Catholic Bishops and Nuclear War*, ed. Judith A. Dwyer, s.s.j (Washington D.C.: Georgetown University Press, 1984), which also includes Michael Novak, 'The U.S. Bishops, The U.S. Government, and Reality'.
3. 'Augustine's Political Realism', *Christian Realism and Political Problems*, p. 159. His Gifford Lectures, *The Nature and Destiny of Man*, 2 Vols. provided the 'theological frame' for his realism, as he noted in *Man's Nature and His Communities*, p. 23.
4. *Man's Nature and His Communities*, p. 22.
5. See *Nature and Destiny of Man*. Vol. 1; 'Reply to Interpretation and Criticism', in *Reinhold Niebuhr*, ed. Kegley, p. 513.
6. Hans J. Morgenthau, 'The Influence of Reinhold Niebuhr in American Life and Thought', and Niebuhr's 'Response', in *Reinhold Niebuhr: A Prophetic Voice in Our Time*, ed. Harold R. Landon (Greenwich, Conn,: The Seabury Press, 1962), pp. 102, 122.
7. Niebuhr, 'The Problem of a Protestant Social Ethic', *Union Seminary Quarterly Review* 15 (November 1959): 10–11. This important article has been neglected in discussions and anthologies of Niebuhr's thought.
8. *Man's Nature and His Communities*, and 'Toward New Intra-Christian Endeavors', *Christian Century* 86 (December 31, 1969): 13–14.
9. 'The Problem of a Protestant Social Ethic', p. 8, first emphasis added.
10. *Moral Man and Immoral Society*, p. 170.

11. 'The Problem of a Protestant Social Ethic', p. 9; see Niebuhr, 'The Development of a Social Ethic in the Ecumenical Movement', and 'Theology and Political Thought in the Western World', *Faith and Politics*, ed. Ronald H. Stone (New York: George Braziller, 1968). pp. 55 and 177. See also the discussion in Landon, ed., *Reinhold Niebuhr*, p. 91. The connection between realism and pragmatism is clear in Niebuhr's statement: 'to know both the law of love as the final standard and the law of self-love as a persistent force is to enable Christians to have a foundation for a pragmatic ethic in which power and self-interest are used, beguiled, harnessed and deflected for the ultimate end of establishing the highest and most inclusive possible community of justice and order' [Niebuhr, 'Christian Faith and Social Action', *Christian Faith and Social Action*, ed. John A. Hutchinson (New York: Charles Scribner's Sons, 1953), p. 241]. Over the years Niebuhr used several different terms such as 'norms', 'laws', ideals', 'standards', and 'principles' very loosely and interchangeably, in part because of his polemical context. For example, the language of ideals pervaded *An Interpretation of Christian Ethics*, which criticized the Social Gospel for its impossible ideals, while the language of norms and principles was prominent in most of his writings in the 1950s and 1960s.
12. 'The Problem of a Protestant Social Ethic', p. 10.
13. Niebuhr, 'Response,' in *Reinhold Niebuhr*, ed. Landon, p. 122.
14. 'The Problem of a Protestant Social Ethic', p. 10.
15. See *Nature and Destiny of Man*, Vol. II, chaps 3 & 9.
16. 'Pacifism Against the Wall' (1936), *Love and Justice*, ed. D. B. Robertson (Cleveland: The World Publishing Co., Meredian Books, 1967), p. 267.
17. 'The Problem of a Protestant Social Ethic', p. 11.
18. 'Is Peace or Justice the Goal?' *World Tomorrow* 15 (September 21, 1932): 276–77, quoted in *Reinhold Niebuhr on Politics*, ed. Harry R. Davis and Robert C. Good (New York: Charles Scribner's Sons, 1960), p. 141. See also *Moral Man and Immoral Society*, p. 240.
19. 'Just or Holy?' *Christianity and Crisis* 1, no. 19 (November 3, 1941): 1.
20. For example, in affirming position (ii), John Howard Yoder holds that the Christian is not responsible for using violence to make history come out right because God is in control, and, in affirming position (iii), Paul Ramsey invokes God's responsibility for history to argue against violating the principle of discrimination. See John Howard Yoder, *The Original Revolution: Essays on Christian Pacifism* (Scottdale, PA: Herald Press, 1971), pp. 132–47; Paul Ramsey, *Deeds and Rules in Christian Ethics* (New York: Charles Scribner's Sons, 1967), pp. 108–109; *The Just War: Force and Political Responsibility* (New York: Charles Scribner's Sons, 1968).
21. 'Pacifism and the Use of Force' (1928). *Love and Justice*, p. 248. John Bennett writes, 'I cannot find that Niebuhr was ever in theory consistently an absolute pacifist'. Bennett, 'Reinhold Niebuhr's Social Ethics', *Reinhold Niebuhr*, ed. Kegley, p. 118.
22. 'Christian Faith and Natural Law' (1940), *Love and Justice*, p. 53. He

also contended that 'only if one adopts the principle that it is better to suffer injustice than to resort to force can one wholly disavow the use of force'. 'Is There Another Way?' (1955), *Love and Justice*, p. 300.

23. On war as the *ultima ratio*, see *Love and Justice*, pp. 192, 296, 300. For an analysis and assessment of Niebuhr's interpretation of violence as the *ultima ratio*, see James F. Childress, *Moral Responsibility in Conflicts: Essays on Nonviolence, War, and Conscience* (Baton Rouge, LA: Louisiana State University Press, 1982), chap. 2.

24. Reinhold Niebuhr and Hans Morgenthau, 'The Ethics of War and Peace in the Nuclear Age' (Informal Discussion), *War/Peace Report* (February 1967): 5.

25. See James F. Childress, *Moral Responsibility in Conflicts*, esp. chap. 3; Ralph Potter, *War and Moral Discourse* (Richmond, VA.: John Knox Press, 1969); James T. Johnson, *Can Modern Wars Be Just?* (New Haven, Conn: Yale University Press, 1984); National Conference of Catholic Bishops, *The Challenge of Peace: God's Promise and Our Response* (Washington, D.C: U.S. Catholic Conference, 1983).

26. James T. Johnson, *Just War Tradition and the Restraint of War* (Princeton, N.J: Princeton University Press, 1981), p. 337. People tend to formulate and use criteria that are analogous to just-war criteria whenever it is impossible to meet all of the moral demands in a situation and it is necessary to compromise or sacrifice some of them. See Childress, *Moral Responsibility in Conflicts*, chap 3.

27. Angus Dun and Reinhold Niebuhr, 'God Wills Both Justice and Peace', *Christianity and Crisis* 15 (June 13, 1955): 77; 'The Problem of a Protestant Social Ethic', p. 8.

28. See *Man's Nature and His Communities*. For Paul Ramsey's appropriation of the just-war tradition, see *War and the Christian Conscience: How Shall Modern War Be Conducted Justly?* (Durham, N.C: Duke University Press, 1961). Ramsey affirms political realism within the limits set by the principle of discrimination and criticizes realism's consequentialist tendencies.

29. For Niebuhr's opposition to the war in Vietnam, see Niebuhr and Morgenthau, 'The Ethics of War and Peace in the Nuclear Age.' Justification also implies limitation.

30. Joseph C. McKenna, S.J., 'Ethics and War: A Catholic View', *American Political Science Review* 54 (1960): 650.

31. 'The Problem of a Protestant Social Ethic', p. 8.

32. Dun and Niebuhr, 'God Wills Both Justice and Peace', p. 78.

33. Niebuhr and Morgenthau, 'The Ethics of War and Peace in the Nuclear Age', and Niebuhr, 'The Problem of a Protestant Social Ethic', p. 8.

34. 'The Problem of a Protestant Social Ethic', p. 8.

35. 'Love Your Enemies' (1942), *Love and Justice*, p. 220. He also distinguished between evil and the embodiment of evil.

36. 'Why I Leave the F.O.R.' (1934), *Love and Justice*, p. 258.

37. See J. Glenn Gray, *The Warriors: Reflections on Men in Battle* (New York: Harper and Row, 1970).

38. Dun and Niebuhr, 'God Wills Both Justice and Peace', p. 78.

39. He used the language of 'indiscriminate' even though he did not clearly accept and explicate the principle of discrimination, at least as an absolute principle.

40. 'The Bombing of Germany' (1943). *Love and Justice*, p. 222, emphasis added. Niebuhr distinguished antecedent guilt (e.g. partial guilt for the emergence of the evil that is being opposed), concomitant guilt (e.g. causing suffering to the innocent), and consequent guilt (e.g. vindictiveness in victory).

41. *Ibid*, p. 223.

42. 'Airplanes Are Not Enough' (1944), *Love and Justice*, p. 190.

43. 'Is the Bombing Necessary?' *Christianity and Crisis* 4, no. 5 (April 3, 1944): 1-2; John C. Ford, S.J., 'The Morality of Obliteration Bombing', *Theological Studies* 5 (1944): 261-309, reprinted in *War and Morality*, ed. Richard Wasserstrom (Belmont, CA: Wadsworth Publishing Co., 1970).

44. See Ramsey, *The Just War*, p. 430.

45. Joseph Fletcher, *Situation Ethics* (Philadelphia: The Westminster Press, 1965).

46. Michael Walzer, *Just and Unjust Wars* (New York: Basic Books, 1977), chap. 16; Walzer, 'World War Two: Why Was This War Different?' *Philosophy and Public Affairs* I (Fall 1971): 3-21.

47. 'To Prevent the Triumph of An Intolerable Tyranny' (1940), *Love and Justice*, p. 275, emphasis added.

48. Walzer, *Just and Unjust Wars*, pp. 323-27; see also Walzer, 'Political Action: The Problem of Dirty Hands', *Philosophy and Public Affairs* 2 (Winter 1973): 160-80.

49. On 'moral traces', see Robert Nozick, 'Moral Complications and Moral Structures', *Natural Law Forum* 13 (1968): 1-50; on 'residual effects', see A. C. Ewing, *Second Thoughts in Moral Philosophy* (London: Routledge and Kegan Paul, 1959), p. 110.

50. By contrast, Paul Ramsey agrees with Joseph Fletcher that the 'lesser evil' is the same as the 'greatest good' possible and 'therefore better characterized as the good or the right thing to do'. Ramsey continues: 'Well do I remember D. C. Macintosh making this same logically compelling point at the onset of Niebuhrian Christian realism. This is still the mood: going about responsibly doing the greatest good possible, and gaining a general sense of guiltiness by calling it the lesser evil. . . It can only confuse ethics if in order to aggravate our sense of sinfulness we *insist* on calling the greatest possible good the lesser evil (which, of course, it is tragically, but not immorally).' Ramsay, *Deeds and Rules in Christian Ethics*, p. 197. As Ramsey indicates, one question is whether Niebuhr conflates questions of physical evil and moral evil.

51. Hans Morgenthau, 'The Influence of Reinhold Niebuhr', p. 106-107.

52. 'The Atomic Bomb' (1945), *Love and Justice*, pp. 232-35.

53. Report of the Commission on the Relation of the Church to the War in the Light of the Christian Faith, appointed by the Federal Council of the Churches of Christ in America, *Atomic Warfare and the Christian Faith*, March, 1946. Although Niebuhr sometimes appeared to deny the

possibility of national repentance for actions, in other contexts he recognized its possibility and importance, noting, for example, how difficult the US atomic bombings had made it for Japan to repent. See 'The Problem of a Protestant Social Ethic', p. 11, and 'The Atomic Bomb', p. 233-34.

54. Landon, ed. *Reinhold Niebuhr*, p. 123.
55. *The Irony of American History*, p. 157.
56. 'The Problem of a Protestant Social Ethic', p. 8.
57. James Johnson, *Just War Tradition and the Restraint of War*, p. 337; contrast John Bennett, 'Reinhold Niebuhr's Social Ethics', p. 137.
58. Niebuhr and Morgenthau, 'The Ethics of War and Peace in the Nuclear Age', p. 4.
59. June Bingham, *Courage to Change* (New York: Scribner's, 1961), p. 386; Bennett, 'Reinhold Niebuhr's Social Ethics', p. 138.
60. Niebuhr, 'The Nuclear Dilemma - A Discussion', *Christianity and Crisis* 21, No. 19 (November 13, 1961): 202, quoted in Bennett, 'Reinhold Niebuhr's Contribution to Christian Social Ethics', *Reinhold Niebuhr*, ed. Landon, p. 78.
61. 'The Problem of a Protestant Political Ethic', *Christian Century* 77 (September 21, 1960): 1085-87.
62. Quoted in Bennett, 'Reinhold Niebuhr's Contribution to Christian Social Ethics', p. 78.
63. 'The Hydrogen Bomb' (1950), *Love and Justice*, pp. 235-37.
64. Paul Ramsey, *The Just War*, pp. 252-58; he later retracted this position: 'I now think that an input of deliberate ambiguity about the counter-people use of nuclear weapons is not possible unless it is (immorally) meant, and not a very good idea in the first place' [Ramsey, 'A Political Ethics Context for Strategic Thinking', *Strategic Thinking and its Moral Implications*, ed. Morton A. Kaplan (Chicago: University of Chicago Center for Policy Study, 1973), p. 142]. National Conference of Bishops, *The Challenge of Peace*; Walzer, *Just and Unjust Wars*, chap. 17.
65. Dun and Niebuhr, 'God Wills Both Justice and Peace', p. 78.
66. *Ibid.*
67. 'The Moral Insecurity of our Security', *Christianity and Crisis* 17, no. 23 (January 6, 1958): 177; for a different emphasis, see 'The Christian Conscience and Atomic War', *Christianity and Crisis* 10, no. 21 (December 11, 1950): 161.
68. See John Keegan, 'The Spectre of Conventional War', *Harper's*, July 1983.
69. Ian Clark, *Limited Nuclear War* (Princeton, N.J: Princeton University Press, 1982), pp. 224-25. For 'command and control' problems, see Paul Bracken, *The Command and Control of Nuclear Forces* (New Haven, Conn.: Yale University Press, 1983).
70. Charles Krauthammer, 'On Nuclear Morality', *Nuclear Arms: Ethics, Strategy, Politics*, ed. R. James Woolsey (San Francisco: Institute for Contemporary Studies Press, 1984), p. 21.
71. National Conference of Bishops, *The Challenge of Peace*, 159.
72. 'Ten Fateful Years', *Christianity and Crisis* 11, no.1 (February 5, 1951): 1.

73. 'The Case for Coexistence', *The New Leader* 37 (October 4, 1954): 5.
74. Niebuhr and Morgenthau, 'The Ethics of War and Peace in the Nuclear Age', p. 5.
75. 'Christian Faith and Social Action', p. 229.
76. Kenneth Thompson, 'The Political Philosophy of Reinhold Niebuhr', *Reinhold Niebuhr*, ed. Kegley, p. 249.
77. Davis and Good, eds. *Reinhold Niebuhr on Politics*, p. 327.

* This chapter was prepared while the author was a Guggenheim Fellow and a Fellow at the Woodrow Wilson International Center for Scholars. He expresses his gratitude to both the Guggenheim Foundation and the Wilson Center for their support.

Reinhold Niebuhr as Political Theologian

LANGDON GILKEY

There can be little question that Reinhold Niebuhr is to be called a 'political theologian'. The major passion that from beginning to end animated both his life and his writings was the passion for social justice; and the major theoretical question he puzzled over all of his life was the question of understanding human beings so as to understand why they behaved in their social relations as they did – and so how the quest for justice might more fruitfully be carried on. His concern later for theology and philosophy of history grew out of and were always subordinate to this primary interest in justice and the social ethics it implied. His major course on his own theology offered at Union Seminary in the late forties was entitled 'Theological Framework for Christian Ethics'. All this is well known.

So powerful, however, has proved the later theological interpretation of social existence, especially his doctrines of human nature, of sin, of grace and of history – for which he is justly famous[1] – that this later theological construction remains for most of us 'Niebuhr', and the earlier works are, therefore, read primarily as merely preparatory. As a consequence it is Niebuhr the theologian who is contrasted, favourably and unfavourably, with current political and liberation theologies. This is well and good; and this author has written a good sized article on just that subject.[2] The present article, therefore, is going to try something else. It seeks to uncover what Niebuhr's political theology was like before it led to and was reshaped by his mature Christian theology. To do this I shall examine his two major 'pre-theological' books: *Moral Man and Immoral Society* and *Reflections on the End of an Era*, to see what he had then to say about social life and its relation to justice.

We shall find Niebuhr here clearly a political theologian – if we can call him in these writings a 'theologian' at all! His only concern is the political (or social) life of humans and how that life can be made more just. His interest in social theories, philosophy or religion is clearly subordinate to that central concern. In many respects, therefore, he has much in common with current political and liberation theologies. He argues repeatedly that revolutionary action, force, is necessary for important social change. Further, he is in a way a Marxist, that is, he applauds and uses much of its theory. He has a decided 'tilt towards the oppressed'; and he regards the dominant capitalist and imperialist society of the West as inevitably doomed and to be replaced by socialist societies. All of this sets him very close to much of present-day liberation theology; in fact most of them are more implicitly or explicitly theological than he is at this point. But there are also differences, differences that lead towards the later theology that seems, and is, so different from contemporary political theologies. This article does not attempt an explicit comparison; it describes only Niebuhr's thought. But I will try to highlight those points where these similarities and differences begin clearly to appear and will comment on them. Let us start with the first of these two major pre-theological political writings: *Moral Man and Immoral Society*.

★   ★   ★   ★   ★

The dominant theses of this justly famous volume[3] are well known. I shall summarize them to provide the basis for an overall picture of Niebuhr's political theology. First, there are the four major theses or themes establishing Niebuhr's fundamental position from thence onward. The last of these (groups are less moral than individuals) is the one usually highlighted; but to me the other three are more basic to Niebuhr's total view and just as new to the optimistic liberal thought of the 1920s and '30s.

(1) *The Ambiguity of Power*

Politics represents a contest of interested power rather than a debate about theories; it is constituted by a struggle of social wills rather than a clash of minds; it is therefore dominated by the interest of groups (5) (now largely economic interest) not by the intellectual curiosity of the wise. This interest is stubborn and resourceful; Niebuhr refers to it as 'the inertia of nature', as 'natural impulse' rather than 'mind'; and he is certain it will always be there – as it is there, hidden but still dominant, in the injustices and conflicts of present bourgeois culture. Such interest represents the real impediment to the achievement of justice, not wrong theory or lack of education (233-34); it is also creative of injustice. For when a group through its function gains predominant power, it appropriates excess rewards and privileges to itself; unequal power therefore results in unequal justice (7). In the end this accrual of power and privilege is so excessive it destroys itself – for it breeds resentment in its victims, the oppressed, and in the end they revolt (81).

Power, however, is not intrinsically evil, nor should it be shunned by the moralist. It is an aspect of 'nature' and as essential for social health as it is creative of its unhealth. To believe it can be eliminated or repudiated is middle class hypocrisy. The privileges of the middle class are dependent on the hidden power and force of the established order; thus for them to condemn the use of power is simply to condemn the explicit use of power by revolutionary groups while condoning the implicit power that keeps the present system of privileges going. Power is necessary to establish unity and order in a community; but it is always *a* group that establishes that unity; and so every achievement of order is saturated with injustice since each ruling group arrogates to itself more privileges than it deserves. Thus, paradoxically, the power necessary to control the wicked is the danger, not the wicked!

Power is also necessary to effect social change and thus to achieve a more tolerable justice. No group voluntarily relinquishes its power – a Niebuhrian theme rehearsed endlessly in these two books (e.g. 34, 121, 130–31, 195). Thus their superior power must be dislodged in the end by opposing force since ruling classes resist loss of power with all the means available to them. Revolutionary action is therefore both necessary and legitimate in the name of justice (129, 146, 171–75). Niebuhr will later repeat this same argument in his defence of the use of force in the war on fascism.

(2) *The Ambiguity of Reason*

While power was wrongly (for Niebuhr) negated by the liberal intellectuals, reason was for him equally wrongly celebrated by them as increasingly dominant in the social sphere. To Niebuhr both power and reason are 'ambiguous' in our common life, capable of positive and negative use alike. To be sure, surprisingly enough for the early Niebuhr reason is the central principle of human creativity, of morals and of hope. It represents the transcending and self-transcending principle that can organize impulse and criticize it, and thus does it represent the universal rather than the particular (25-33). Modern savants, however, have overemphasized this critical, organizing and universalizing role of reason. Probably because their professional work enacts it, they 'live off it'; further, since they are middle class intellectuals, the irrational, predatory and impulsive nature of social life has effectively been kept hidden from them. They fail to see both the impulsive nature of social life and the predatory use of reason within it. For reason is also ambiguous: it is frequently used by any powerful group to justify its dubious actions in pursuit of its interests. Dominant groups are, therefore, essentially characterized by *hypocrisy*, the rational pretence that their dominance is justified (117). 'The will to power uses reason, as kings use chaplains and courtiers, to add grace to their enterprises.' (44). But reason does more than justify impulse. It extends, strengthens and transmutes natural impulse into a far more lethal power. Through reason, by which the natural human being becomes self-aware and so aware of its own mortality, the limited will to survive of the animal world becomes the unlimited will to power of the human; thus 'mind sharpens nature's claws'. (44). Here lie the seeds of Niebuhr's most fundamental later theological insight: the relation of 'spirit' to anxiety and thence to the subsequent idolatry of self and of group that he terms 'pride' and which constitutes the major ingredient of social sin.

(3) *The Ambiguity of Religion*
This is also an essential Niebuhrian category and one equally alien to the liberal tradition in religious thought. Niebuhr defines religion as a sense for the Absolute (note the Schleiermachian not Ritschlian definition despite Niebuhr's clear affinity to Ritschl's

theology.) At this stage Niebuhr writes about religion almost as if he considered it to be thoroughly a human projection. He speaks without qualification of 'religion investing the cosmos with ethical will', and so on (52–53). Later, religion will be clearly termed a *response*, both to the universal divine presence and to revelation (cf. *Nature and Destiny of Man* Vol I, 125–49). Throughout, however, Niebuhr is clear on the ambiguity of religion. On the one hand profound religion relativizes the ego and the group – in which case its characteristic danger is to relativize and so to swallow up all moral distinctions (66–67). (Interestingly, Augustine is here criticized as a 'pessimist', whereas later he will, on just this same point of transcendence, be held up as a paradigm.) But religion can also give ultimacy to the partial ego by identifying the latter with the absolute (65–66). Profound religion, however, is invaluable, for in its search for the transcendent it can both relativize the immediate and yet sense its true value, be realistic about it and yet committed to and hopeful about a transcendent standard (80–82). This dialectic of transcendence and immanence will, of course, become fundamental for Niebuhr's later interpretation of revelation, of judgement and grace, and so to his understanding of God's activities in history.

(4) *The Immorality of Groups*

This theme runs throughout the book although in the end the sharp distinction between individual and group 'virtue' is less crucial than the other themes mentioned. However, Niebuhr clearly wished to emphasize this distinction, if only to prevent optimistic liberal views of individual rationality and morality from deluding us about collective behaviour. Groups have, Niebuhr feels, almost no possibilities for moral action, and individuals have little enough! (e.g. 107). There can be no transcendence of the group by critical reason nor any subordination of its interests to a wider universal interest (88, 107). There are two major reasons for this: (a) there is no self-transcending consciousness in group life. The ruling clique or oligarchy does not represent the whole in self-awareness but one specific interest within the group; it is no closer to the universal than is any other faction (88). (b) Each individual conscience sees itself as 'moral' when it subordinates its personal interests to the larger, 'universal' interests of the group, and especially when it defends the group. Thus is the altruism of individuals cajoled into contributing to the egoism of the group: 'the unselfishness of individuals makes for the selfishness of nations' (91); and 'a combination of unselfishness and vicarious selfishness in the individual thus gives tremendous force to national egoism' (95). (One notes that even here no absolute distinction is made between individual and group selfishness.) As a result the group is characterized by hypocrisy; for individual standards of morality are offended at the group's egoism and must be appeased even if they cannot be obeyed. Groups, therefore, claim to represent universal values, and thus can they keep the moral assent as well as the egoistic devotion of their members (97). Needless to say, this analysis of egoism, universal claims and hypocrisy laid the foundation for the later categories of idolatry and self-deception so crucial to Niebuhr's theological interpretation of sin, an interpretation which included both individual and corporate human existence. Here, however, this analysis is largely confined to his description of nations and of privileged classes.

Although as in the above case Niebuhr frequently speaks of nations, there is little question that the main groups Niebuhr has in mind, even in the next volume also, are classes and that the primary social conflicts are class conflicts. He is convinced that economic power is the central form of social power (89–90, 210); that economic injustice is more fundamental than is political injustice; and that therefore the levelling of economic privilege and power remains the central task for modern society, if it would achieve greater justice (163–64). Thus is the communist oligarch, who possesses merely political power, less a threat than the capitalist one who possesses both forms of power (90). Since it is Marxism that has pointed all this out, it remains, despite its several (if intelligible) errors of 'overemphasis' (162, 164), the truest social philosophy available – and any Christian social ethic must take full account of it. While Niebuhr's 'determinism' is more evident in the next volume, still it is clear that he understands history as in accord with Marxist hopes: socialism is inevitably to be the next stage of development of Western society (144). One can only hope, he says, that the urgency of their vision will be tempered with more tolerance and more confidence in moral and religious forces than they show at present. However, their materialistic determinism and their cynicism, while misleading, are understandable (155): they see the real mechanistic brutalities of a pious and moralistic bourgeois culture (105–106); and their absolutizing of their own class as history's saviour is intelligible as the action of an oppressed group (156–57).

Not only is Niebuhr here clearly influenced by Marxist thought; he also has what liberation theologians have called a 'tilt towards the oppressed' – though not on any explicit Christian basis. First, he is convinced that only the oppressed can see the truth in a social situation since they alone, who suffer from them, are aware of the brutalities and conflicts present there, of the struggles of interest and power that characterize society (151, 157, 165–67). Correspondingly, the upper classes – and their 'chaplains', the social scientists – cannot see social reality (113, 233). (a) They are fooled by the mechanical and rational relations of bourgeois life and so miss the contest of power beneath the surface; and (b) they must deceive themselves about the society that grants them inordinate privileges, and so they identify this dubious and brutal order with a just, or even a divine, order so that they are morally justified in defending it (129). (c) By applying the standards appropriate for individuals to society as a whole, they also condemn violent action against that order – at the same time calling on police and army to defend it (129–30, 176). The oppressed alone, therefore, see society's ambiguity truly; their only 'fault' is consistently to overlook the possibility of tolerance, justice, rationality and ethical goodwill in other classes that might support them and whose help they need both to rule and to rule justly.

Niebuhr is also clear that the oppressed alone deserve the active help of relevant social, moral and religious forces. Theirs alone is the cause that it is morally justified to defend in the modern situation: 'A war for the emancipation of a nation, a race or a class is thus placed in a different moral category from the use of power for the perpetuation of imperial rule or class domination. . . . It is important to insist, first of all, that equality is a higher social goal than peace. . . . In this respect Marxian philosophy is more true than pacifism.' (234–35). Niebuhr's fundamental agreement at this stage with much contemporary liberation theology could hardly be more evident.

If we ask what at this stage the implicit differences are with contemporary liberation theologies, I would hazard the following three elements as my answer. These will be elaborated further in our section on *Reflections.*

(a) There is even here a sharp criticism of Marxist thought and practice. Not just that it is atheistic and so 'merely social'. Rather precisely that it is *not.* Niebuhr sees it as fundamentally a religion (154–60). As he says later, 'It detests Christianity with all the hatred of one religion for a rival and of irreligion for religion' (*Reflections,* 193). Marxism is based on a myth held in faith, and thus like all religions it is ambiguous unless it is self-critical. But this it is not, and on its own terms it cannot be. Because it is too dogmatic, it ignores the dangers of political power, it is saturated with many of the illusions of modern liberal technological culture, and above all it absolutizes the claims and prejudices of its own class – and thus has neither understanding nor pity for other classes (192–95). This critique will sharpen as the decade from 1932 to 1940 unfolds.

(b) Niebuhr is continuously interested in understanding human being as well as implementing ethical practice; certainly the latter remains central, but still he seems, as did Marx, to be convinced that effective political action depends on valid political understanding, insight or theory – and thus he is deeply concerned to understand rightly. Clearly Niebuhr is searching for insight into *why* we behave as we do, and as a consequence at this period he is exploring different categories for interpreting our social existence. If privileged classes and dominant nations behave as they do, why do they do so? In answer we find categories such as 'impulse', 'nature', 'will to power', etc. appearing to undergird his theory of class and national interest and conflict and so to give theoretical foundation for a realistic and so effective ethic aimed at justice. These categories change, as we shall note; but one important result of this interest in understanding and in valid theory is that the *bases* of social behaviour are by him driven back into human nature itself. As a consequence, out of his social analysis and ethic of praxis is appearing an *anthropology*. And because of this 'empirical' process, it is an anthropology not ready-made, provided by either liberalism, orthodoxy or Marxism. On the contrary it is one developed empirically, out of the processes of his own inquiry into and reflection upon social conflicts and human behaviour. It should be noted as a methodological aside that every one of the conclusions about human nature, society, history or religion which we have rehearsed in connection with either volume, is 'empirical' and not 'theological'; that is, they are based solely on Niebuhr's observation of historical and social behaviour rather than on scripture, tradition or inherited doctrine.

(c) The same is even more true of the philosophy of history slowly taking shape here. It is barely visible in this volume; it will be more evident and again more developed, if also more confused and incoherent, in *Reflections.* The big change between this 'pre-theological' period and the period of Niebuhr's mature theology (1935–49) lies in the development of these two aspects of theology: an anthropology and a view of history – and the views of revelation, God, grace and eschatology that they implied and so that were part of Niebuhr's total view. This new theological anthropology and theology of history (his mature view) are significantly different from the explicit anthropology and philosophy of history in these two volumes before us. Yet the 'seeds' of these new viewpoints are there, as we have noted. And the presence of these 'seeds', these intimations of what is to come, plus the theoretical interest we have just mentioned, is together what sharply differentiates Niebuhr at this stage from liberation theologies. To be more precise, Niebuhr all along is working out his own view of human nature and of history, and working it out over against all the other available viewpoints: liberal social thought, Marxism, liberal Christian thought and orthodoxy. Seemingly all given theories are for him in flux and will be so until the new theological understanding appears. In contrast (so it seems to me) either the Marxist analysis of society or an eschatological theology of history seem to be 'given' to much of contemporary theology – and thus do they end up with a quite different social and political perspective.

★   ★   ★   ★   ★

Most of the large themes outlined above continue in *Reflections on the End of an Era.*[4] That social existence represents a conflict of interest and of power, a conflict that can never be fully eliminated; that reason 'is the servant of impulse before it is its master' (17); that in collective behaviour reason serves largely to rationalize group egoism, and thus is it inadequate to create justice; that religion, while necessary as inciting the quest for justice and as providing the framework for social insight, is ambiguous (183–84) – these remain constant as the main constitutive elements of Niebuhr's view of politics.

The emphasis on class conflict as the key to social history also continues. The rise of fascism is, as it was by so many in the early 1930s, interpreted largely as the defence by the ruling classes of capitalism against communism, a 'delirious' effort by the capitalist owners to preserve their social power and dominance (60–61). Niebuhr's question, therefore, is: will the workers continue to be deluded enough to join, quite against their own interests, the already 'confused' lower middle classes in this frantic last defence of capitalist ownership? Niebuhr feels that they will, but that the war that fascism will inevitably produce will

itself in turn lead to the victory of socialism throughout the West (30–35, 56–61, 81–83, 165–67; and cf also
Moral Man 190f.). Niebuhr's own *actual* reaction to
fascism, and to the war against it, from 1938–45,
namely to have a new and deeper appreciation of
democracy, was to prove quite different from this predicted outcome of fascism leading to an ultimate communist victory in the then capitalist states – though his
earlier prediction that communism would win in
'agrarian Asia' was right on target! (*Moral Man* 191) In
any case, the dynamics of social change are still seen
primarily in terms of the struggles of its economic
classes, and clearly the 'workers' are viewed as the
bearers of the ultimate social ideal towards which the
'logic of history' is moving (141–48, 160–61).

Certain less familiar themes are, moreover, enlarged.
For example, there is Niebuhr's view that the theoretical structures of an era (its social theories, philosophical viewpoints, even some of its religious or
theological views) are largely shaped by the character
of the economic social relations in that era. Niebuhr
cites several cases: the derivation of the philosophy of
individualism from the new social and economic relations of urban life (91–92); the derivation of liberal
rational ethics from the 'mechanistic and rational relations' of modern technological and commercial society
(66, 112); and finally the origination of Marxism's
determinism and atheism (and that of naturalistic liberalism) in the same 'mechanical and rational' relations of modern industrial life (196). Correspondingly,
the theme of the 'blindness' of the bourgeois class and
of its 'wise men', the social scientists, to the realities
of social existence is expanded into a much more
detailed critique of liberal social theory. The automatic
and rational mechanisms of commerce and finance
obscure the reality of the contest for power (4),
delude the 'scientific' observer into a naive faith in

social harmony created out of the 'harmless ego' and prudent 'reason' of the bourgeois executive, and result in the illusory optimism of liberal theory – just when the conflicts of modern society reach their climax. As Niebuhr puts this irony: 'Destined to premature decay, it (bourgeois culture) dreamed of progress almost until the hour of its dissolution' (3); and 'With rather pathetic irony modern civilization proceeded to tear itself asunder in its conflicts between nations and classes while modern culture dreamed of perpetual peace' (14). The sense of catastrophy, of the tragic dimension to historical life, as well as the possibility of something quite new arising out of the death of the old, seemed evident enough to him; and yet all were quite obviously lacking in liberal culture. His political realism continues unabated, or, if anything, deepened.

★   ★   ★   ★   ★

What is it, then, that is new in *Reflections?* How is his political philosophy developing? Even if his thought is not yet 'theological' – in the sense of using explicitly Christian symbols to interpret historical life – is it moving in that direction? If we can answer these questions, then perhaps more light will be shed on the similarities and differences of Niebuhr's political theology with contemporary versions of such theology.

The first thing one notices is that concurrent with, and explanatory of, the above analysis of society, its ills and its prospects, Niebuhr is spending even more time developing, or beginning to develop, an anthropology and a philosophy of history. Both of these are as yet inchoate; or, more accurately, because of the originality and depth of his social insights, they represent at this point an uneasy and clearly unstable confusion. His earlier views on each of these subjects: the nature of human being and the dynamic processes of history, are now being increasingly placed under pressure or strain by his own developing understanding of the dynamics of society. The earlier categories he had used for his analysis still remain; his later theological symbols or categories have not at all appeared. But these earlier categories (e.g. nature, impulse, reason etc.) are obviously shifting; their new content, so to speak, is bursting them open and frequently contradicting their original intent. Like the history he sees before him, his earlier 'theories' of human being and of history – such as they are – are undergoing challenge and revision; and soon something quite new will appear. What is new, therefore, in *Reflections* is the clarity with which this confusion of past interpretation with present insight can be seen, and the way in which that confusion presages and calls for the later theological interpretation.

The developed theology of his mature works appears, therefore (just as Niebuhr frequently said), in order 'to make sense' of the confusions and irrationalities of common experience, confusions which the categories of liberal theory were quite unable to handle. Although he does not say as much, it is clear that Niebuhr's developed thought represents a 'correlation' between the 'facts of experience' (as he liked to term them) on the one hand and the cohering, illuminating power of theological symbols. For in Niebuhr's thought it is all of *this* that we will have gone through in these two volumes that the 'biblical symbols' later cohere and interpret in his developed theology. At this point this correlation has not yet happened because the biblical symbols have not yet appeared. However, we can (with hindsight) see Niebuhr's thought moving towards them, at least in the sense that the old categories are being burst asunder by his developing social insights.

Let us begin with anthropology. Niebuhr still uses

the categories inherited from his liberal background. On the one hand there is 'nature' with its 'impulses'. These characterize and dominate human social existence: 'Our optimistic rationalists fail to recognize that the collective enterprises of man belong to the order of nature more than to the order of reason' (31); and thus the 'parable of the jungle' gives a truer picture of the life and death of civilizations. Over against impulse is 'reason'. Niebuhr disagrees with 'rationalists' when they hold that mind can be dominant over impulse in social life, but he does not yet disagree enough to insist (as he later would) that this conventional dualism of nature and reason is inappropriate for the proper delineation of human behaviour (cf. e.g. 4–9).

These 'dualist' categories, however, are already tending to shift and to become confused as his analysis proceeds deeper. He sees even more clearly than in the previous volume that it is reason that enlarges natural impulse into human aggression. Through reason humans sense their mortality and thus are led, and enabled, to subordinate other life to the needs of their own security (6–7); through reason aggression is rationalized so as to be acceptable to the conscience. Reason transmutes the will to live into the human will to power (6, 8); and then it hides the latter with its own ideal covering. Thus impulse is no longer mere impulse; nor is reason any longer the dependable principle of order and justice. In sorting these paradoxes out, Niebuhr suggests that the power of reason to subordinate impulse to the universal be called 'spirit', and the power of reason to enhance impulse into aggression be called 'nature' (9). Somewhat ruefully he admits that both are 'myths' since in both cases 'mind' has mixed with 'impulse' to create something quite different from either one (9, 171). And he even utters a sentence inconceivable in the terms of his later theology: 'The task [of justice] must be performed by those who know that the world of history is the world of nature' – though he adds that 'that world has perils of which the world of nature knows nothing' (179). Clearly the later biblical symbols of creature (nature) and *imago dei* (as self-transcending spirit) entered to clarify and reorder this temporary confusion and to straighten out these 'myths'. As noted, this confusion has been caused by Niebuhr's own developing insights that increasingly ran contrary to the intent of his original categories of interpretation.

The same, on perhaps an even larger scale, is happening to Niebuhr's philosophy of history. As we noted, the question of the nature of the processes that characterize history is much more dominant in *Reflections*: the rise and fall of civilizations is this book's main theme. And characteristically he is beginning to develop his own original insights into these processes, insights that will later be transmuted into his mature 'theology of history'. But again he begins with another hermeneutic, another mode of interpreting historical process, in this case one inherited from Marxism. This is a 'deterministic' interpretation, one in which the changes in the structures and the crucial events of historical life unfold irrevocably and inexorably according to a 'logic of history' set by the developments of technology, of industrial patterns and the economic relations resulting from these two. He never makes this view of history explicit; but it appears over and over in the background, as a kind of leitmotiv. One notes it in his references to 'the logic of history' (31, 82, 143), in his use of phrases such as 'bound to' (18, 35), 'certain to' (147, 161), 'inexorable' and 'inevitable' (53, 147, 161) and so on, when he is describing the crises facing capitalism, its development into fascism and the coming appearance of communism in all

industrial societies. Associated with this mild but real
determinist view is the clear sense, which we have
described, of the mission of the proletarian class, the
relative equalizing of fundamental power that public
economic ownership will bring, and so the healing
power of Marxist ideology. At this point it is still true
that for him the socialist interpretation of society is *the*
way to achieve justice – although, as we shall see,
sharper and sharper critiques of these assumptions are
appearing. Much like the dualistic categories of
impulse and mind, this 'radical' philosophy of history
is there, so to speak, as he starts out; it is his 'pre-
understanding'. And again, increasingly it is his own
insights, combined with the historical events of the
middle and late thirties, that first challenge and then
cause him to reformulate this deterministic view of
history as well. (For the sharp contrast with his later
understanding, cf. the following from *The Nature and
Destiny of Man*, Vol. II, 80: 'Where there is history at
all, there is freedom; and where there is freedom,
there is sin.')

What is it, then, that begins the challenge to this
Marxist determinism? In *Reflections* this challenge contains, I think, three elements.

(a) It is interesting that most of the cases where
Niebuhr sees some development in history as 'inevitable', 'certain', 'bound to happen', etc. turn out to be
not the result of changes in economic relations at all
but ways of behaviour which he has found universally
characteristic of humans in collective life. Fascism is
'bound to come' in the West because owners 'are certain to defend' their economic power derivative from
ownership – and 'no privileged class ever voluntarily
resigns its primacy'. Such an act would, he says, be
'contrary to nature'; and thus as a result ruling classes
are 'bound to seek the prolongation of their rule by

the use of pure force'. (e.g. 18, 30, 35, 158). Clearly we are here dealing with what he is later to call the 'inevitabilities of sin' rather than the necessities of a determined historical process. It is an inevitability within freedom not over it, and, as he later said frequently, not a part of any 'logic of history'. But all this remains at this point quite unclarified; and thus is the actual mode of determinism he has in mind, and its relation to any logic of history, unclear. As Niebuhr remarks, Marxism does not know what to do with the puzzle of determinism and freedom (130f) – but I doubt if he saw his own thought at that juncture as an example of just that point!

(b) The second element in the challenge to his initial philosophy of history is the increasing vigour and depth of his critique of Marxism. We have noted the continuation in *Reflections* of many Marxist themes and doctrines. In this volume, however, the critique easily balances the agreement. Niebuhr enlarges on his interpretation of Marxism as religion. Here, he says, is a view of the whole where unconscious forces are held to shape history towards the ideal; thus is it 'myth' (126–35), and like all myths, it is held by faith not scientific inquiry. Also like all religious myths, it deals with the question of the meaning of suffering, with pessimism, and it promises a resolution (193–95). However, while it is relatively true (135), it lacks depth; it has none of the sense, given only by transcendence, of 'the distinction of spirit and nature', and so it ends up with an illusory optimism not essentially different from that of liberalism (136).

An even stronger criticism appears, however, when Niebuhr writes about the spirit of vengeance in the oppressed and the dangers for the quest for justice which this involves. This vindictiveness is quite understandable, he says; the oppressors have resisted change to the end and their oppression has meant untold suffering. Still, this vengeance is deadly to any prospects for real justice. For now the particular sufferings of the oppressed group are identified with *all* suffering; and the particular form of evil represented by the oppressor is identified as the absolute principle of evil itself (i.e. capitalism) (168) – and thus *ipso facto* those oppressed by capitalism do not share at all in that evil, nor do their foes participate in any forms of good at all (169). As a consequence the peasants and the lower middle classes are alike subsumed under the needs and the strategies of the victorious proletariat and so in turn newly oppressed. Moreover, creative elements within even the formerly oppressing class are ignored and scorned. Worst of all, no pity or reconciliation are here possible (169–70). All of this Niebuhr calls 'vindictiveness' (174) – but *what* he is seeing there is what he will later term pride and idolatry, the absolutizing of the self or the group, the creature making itself God and thus aggressing against the neighbour. And even now, Niebuhr sees in it all the characteristics of his later notion of sin. The communist is, says Niebuhr, blind to the similarity of sin in the self as in the opponent (169); he views his own impulses (of vengeance) as instruments of an absolute good (171) and is as a result 'most inhuman'. As a result, they 'reveal the cruelty which always characterizes the will to power of righteous people who are certain they are instruments of a righteous cause' (172). These sentences might have appeared in his later theological writings.

As a consequence, Niebuhr concludes that the absolutizing of the relative by the radical is as dangerous as that done by the conservative (184) – a sentence almost inconceivable from the pen of most liberation theologians. He also points out that this process is not due to capitalism but to the perpetual problem of

group egotism (169); and therefore that the communist oligarch is hardly to be preferred to the capitalist
one (244). Almost all the elements of his later doctrine of sin are evident here: religious idolatry leading
to injustice, i.e. to aggression and cruelty to the neighbour. All of this, however, remains strangely unclarified because it is set within the terms of his older
anthropology which no longer fit, any more than does
his lingering determinist view of history.

One notes throughout this critical discussion of
Marxism (as well as of liberalism) a new appreciation
of religious transcendence. Niebuhr still holds firmly
to the ambiguity of religion; but he seems clearer as
to the value of the transcendent principle latent in
religion ('classical religion' here; later 'prophetic religion'; still later 'biblical faith'). Only on the basis of
such transcendence is it possible to value the particular, to see realistically the depth of its faults, and to
effect a new attitude as well (197). Only here is the
'distinction of nature and spirit clearly seen', and so
the individual affirmed, criticized and yet renewed:
'the consciousness of God and of sin arise together'
(114, 229). Clearly the fundamental terms of Niebuhr's
understanding are shifting from those of liberal analysis (nature and mind) and of Marxism (class, logic of
history, *the* social ideal) to ones founded in some
understanding of religion. Equally clearly the terms or
symbols by which the later interpretation is to be
structured are not yet here. Niebuhr's insights into
social reality have driven him beyond both of these
two 'secular' alternatives – as a result, as his friend
Tillich might have put it, this analysis of the situation
in its disruption 'calls for' the symbols of revelation
which Niebuhr is later to make central.

(c) Niebuhr ends his political analysis with a dual
thesis: (i) that the principle of the balance of power is

the heart of the quest for justice; and (ii) that the radical urge for fundamental change must be tempered by the liberal tolerance of divergent views and aims (251–58). Both represent a new understanding of the political and its requirements, the beginning (on the political level) of the 'new Niebuhr'; but also, as we have tried to show, both are clear fruits of original insights that have increasingly dominated all his work during this crucial decade. In conclusion I shall confine my remarks to the meaning for his political views of this new emphasis on the balance of power.

Niebuhr had, to be sure, always held what might be called a subordinate principle of the balance of power, subordinate, that is, to the principle that economic power is fundamental. Thus while earlier he had said that 'the ultimate social goal' was the eradication of inordinate and special economic power, still he seemed to agree that with that action the issue of justice would be resolved and that new, equally basic, threats to the balance would not occur. Moreover, with economic power central and determinative, democracy, the political expression of a balance of power, remained itself subordinate, in fact he termed it 'a sham', unable, because it dealt only with political power, to challenge or change the more formidable forms of economic power.

In this volume, however, a basic change is represented. The balance of power has become, he now says, the central principle of a radical politics. In effect to me this means the appearance of Niebuhr's developed *political* theory, that which replaces the older framework and so that which, as we have suggested, later is in correlation with his mature theology of politics. Let us spell out what for political theory and for philosophy of history this new emphasis on balance of power means.

(a) First, it means that no particular ideology, no one social arrangement, political or economic, contains either the secret of social understanding or the recipe for social justice. No utopia is possible; and, more of a change, no particular 'blueprint' is absolute. The later Niebuhr is well known for his anti-ideological stance; changeless blueprints, of whatever sort, are more dangerous than helpful in history; history is to be dealt with *pragmatically* if it is to be dealt with creatively. Here begins this theme.

There are, he now sees, variant forms of power dependent on the wide variety of possible societies. The point is that an imbalance of power, and so injustice, can result from *any one* of these. Such an imbalance – of political power in communism, of economic power in capitalism (244) – will result in new forms of injustice, new potential bases for social conflict, and so new modes of tyranny by whatever ruling class organizes the society. Without a check on power in all of its forms, achieved only by continually balancing one form of power against another, *any* form of society can become tyrannical (244). Thus is democracy a permanently necessary aspect of a healthy and just social existence, the *political* basis for renewed justice in any social situation (244). One suspects that Niebuhr's experience of the Russian oligarchy in the early 1930s, and possibly the beginnings of the ascendency of Nazi political power over the capitalistic economic power that tried to contain it, has effected this fundamental shift: economic power is not the only, nor even the only fundamental, form of power, nor the only one that is dangerous.

(b) If the need for a balance of power is permanent because the possibility of some dominant power and so of injustice is permanent, then the source of the problem of injustice lies beyond the issue of the *form* of the society, in fact beyond or beneath both the economic and the political levels of action and of discourse, important as both of those levels are. The source of the problem lies in the 'human', in the character of human nature – since apparently it can infect any political or economic form of society. At this point Niebuhr says 'the root of the conflict . . . is found in the corporate egoism of contending groups' – whatever social entities, classes or ruling cliques they belong to. As we have seen, he has more and more explored this issue, seeking · understanding of it through his 'mythical' categories of nature, mind and spirit. Clearly, therefore, political and economic analyses alike call for a different and deeper level of interpretation if they are to be made intelligible, a level he is later to develop as 'theology', that is, theological anthropology and theology of history. Correspondingly, and much more important, only a religious renewal (repentance and grace), not political action or economic reform, important as they are on their own level, can effect renewal on this new religious level of the problem. Perhaps Niebuhr's greatest theological efforts from now on would be to keep clear the importance and the 'autonomy' of this religious level, and yet *not* thereby to lose the significance and the claim of the political and economic levels (cf. his unsatisfactory but very important distinction between equality of sin and inequality of guilt in *The Nature and Destiny of Man*, Vol. I, chap. 8).

(c) Finally, Niebuhr seems even more clear than before that there is no final solution to the problem of justice. He has, as we have seen, been anti-utopian from the beginning. But his frequent use of the categories of the 'logic of history' and 'an ultimate social ideal' qualified this, at least in principle. Now the sense of the permanence of the problem of justice, the permanence of suffering from injustice and so of the tragedy of catastrophe, have become central to his thought about history (cf. 184–85). He remains (to the surprise of many) a guarded optimist: slow progress is possible, he assures us many times (*Moral Man* 209, 256; *Reflections* 140). But 'every balance of power . . . is a potential chaos which has been coaxed to a momentary cosmos. The chaos will occasionally erupt' (245). As a consequence no society can permanently guarantee either justice or peace: it cannot guarantee justice because some interested oligarchy will rule any society, it will grab inordinate privileges to itself, and it will identify its order with eternal order; and it cannot guarantee peace because such rule, inevitably generating privileges and injustice, creates in its turn suffering and resentment, and so calls in the end for resistance and finally vengeance (246–47).

Clearly some other principle for the meaning of history than the immanent 'logic of historical development' referred to earlier is called for; and evidently that principle must be both more transcendent and more inward, more religious. This transcendence, as he now sees clearly, is necessary to provide grounds for *permanent* criticism or judgement of every *status quo*, to be a principle of hope within continuing catastrophe and tragedy, and through the absoluteness of its ideal, to provide a continuing ground for change and renewal 'beyond tragedy'. Again, we are on our way towards Niebuhr's 'biblical theology'. But already, even without that theology, we have moved far from what most of the current liberation or political theologians would wish to say about either anthropology or philosophy of history.

NOTES

1. Cf. as loci for these doctrines: *Beyond Tragedy; The Nature and Destiny of Man*, Vols I and II; *Faith and History*.
2. 'Niebuhr's Theology of History', in *The Journal of Religion*, vol. 54, number 4 (October, 1974); and reprinted in Nathan A. Scott Jr, ed., *The Legacy of Reinhold Niebuhr*, Chicago, The University of Chicago Press, 1974.
3. *Moral Man and Immoral Society*. (Page references in this section are to this volume in its 1960 edition.)
4. *Reflections on the End of an Era*. (Page references in this section are, unless otherwise stated, all to this volume.)

I can recall my liberal father, a good friend of Niebuhr's, remarking when, in 1932, he first read this book, 'Reinnie's gone crazy!'. Fifteen years later (1947) he told me he had completely changed his mind about the truth of its message. I still have (from him) a copy of a review of *Moral Man* by King Gordon in the *Nation* describing the book 'as an example of medieval monastic gloom. Niebuhr actually says here that a perfect society is not possible in history!'

The Cross and Contemporary Culture

DOUGLAS HALL

1. *Between Two Incongruous Accounts of the World*
Creativity in any field of human endeavour is always
at base a mystery, but it seems to me evident that the
theological contribution of Reinhold Niebuhr is
bound up with a certain fundamental tension
between the faith traditions he appropriated and the
spirit of the culture to which he belonged. His struggle is inseparable from the biographical-historical fact
that he was at the same time thoroughly North American and thoroughly a child of the Protestant Reformation. There are those who would find no 'incongruity'
here, for they regard the United States of America as
the Protestant culture *par excellence*; but while (as
Niebuhr himself frequently noted[1]) the Calvinist influence has certainly been strong in America, the Reformation as it comes to us from the side of Luther has
not. And it was Luther's reformulation of the Faith
that grasped, in a primary sense, the spirit of Reinhold Niebuhr.[2]

Although Lutheranism eventually became relatively
strong on this Continent, few historically important
voices in the formation of the 'New World' spoke out
of Luther's reform. This is due to many practical factors, such as patterns of immigration; but the relative
silence of the Lutheran tradition in the creation of
'America' is due as well to the fact that what was distinctively Lutheran was in many ways at loggerheads
with the whole American experiment. For all his dis-
trust of puny, sinful *anthropos*, Jean Calvin, with his

christocentric triumphalism and his doctrine of election, could rather readily be co-opted by the spirit of an evolving 'Americanism'[3] – as could John Wesley with his moral perfectionism. But Luther, that still-medieval man, steeped in mysticism, given to outlandish pronouncements laced with 'expletives', finding always vast discrepancies between the true *gloria Dei* and the bright designs of empires, insisting upon retaining the Cross as faith's primary focus, and fearing above all what Niebuhr once identified on Luther's behalf as 'the pretension of finality'[4] – this Luther could never find a comfortable home in our brave, new world. In consequence, until our own immediate epoch most American and Canadian Lutherans have kept their faith largely to themselves, nurturing it, often, within rather well-defined ethnic ghettos. Luther's emphases, where they were not sufficiently diluted, seemed thoroughly out of tune with the going world view, like some dark tale belonging to the melancholy gothic caverns of old Europe. Enough to let that tale, suitably personalized by a Hauge or a Grundtvig, inform one's private life and keep one's sons and daughters in touch with a Past that was increasingly foreign to their social milieu.

Reinhold Niebuhr, whose own early life was marked by the generational conflict implicit in this situation, augmented by war with 'the Fatherland', emerged from this crucible as a very rare bird on the American landscape. He had apprehended the essence of the European-made tradition without in the process imbibing its historical *accidens*. Informed in a rudimentary way by the core of this tradition – the 'theology of the cross' – he provided an entirely indigenous expression of it, one which took with complete seriousness the socio-political particularities of the 'New World' context and entered into an ongoing dialogue with the assumptions concealed within them.

This meant that Niebuhr lived at the intersection of what had become history's most 'positive' cultural philosophy and a faith tradition that from the perspective of such a culture could only seem the essence of negativity! 'Pessimism', the charge regularly laid at his doorstep, is of course a naive and simply inaccurate description of Niebuhr's position – as it is of Luther's, Augustine's, Paul's or of the Hebrew prophets and wisdom writers like Job and Koheleth, all of whom contributed substantially to the tradition Niebuhr honoured and himself extended. Yet from the standpoint of an attitude towards historical existence as uncomplicatedly 'positive' as Modernity's, especially in its American adaptation, nothing could have been more predictable than that the truth to which Niebuhr felt himself bound would be deemed consistently 'negative'. After all, he insisted upon discussing Sin in a society that had either reduced that profound biblical concept to bourgeois immorality or else dismissed it altogether. He even dared to reflect upon the life of the human being and human communities along the lines of 'the tragic', and to enucleate a Gospel that could point 'beyond tragedy' – this in a society where, as Rolf Hochhuth put it in his play *Soldiers*, the word 'tragedy' is unknown: 'they call it migraine'.

The rejection of Niebuhr's account of reality by representatives of the official culture and church was very nearly universal.[5] That both Modernists and Fundamentalists should have spurned his rendition of the Christian message was of course to be expected. But even close associates often found him too consistently in a state of continuing struggle – too little sanctified, as it were. Understandably, this reaction to Niebuhr shows up more conspicuously in his early works, before he had become too famous to be held at a distance by persons in his immediate sphere of influence. In a moving entry in his *Leaves From the Note-*

book of a Tamed Cynic, the Detroit pastor ruminates on his relations with a certain friend, 'H':

> Whenever I exchange thoughts with H——— . . . I have the uneasy feeling that I belong to the forces which are destroying religion in the effort to refine it. He is as critical as I am – well, perhaps not quite so critical; but in all his critical evaluations of religious forms he preserves a robust religious vitality which I seem to lack. . . . He has preserved a confidence in the goodness of men and the ultimate triumph of righteousness which I do not lack, but to which I do not hold so unwaveringly. . . .
>
> I have been profoundly impressed by the Spenglerian thesis that culture is destroyed by the spirit of sophistication and I am beginning to suspect that I belong to the forces of decadence in which this sophistication is at work. I have my eye too much upon the limitations of contemporary religious life and institutions; I always see the absurdities and irrationalities in which narrow types of religion issue. . . .
>
> Nevertheless I hate a thoroughgoing cynic. I don't want anyone to be more cynical than I am. If I am saved from cynicism at all it is by some sense of personal loyalty to the spirit and genius of Jesus; that and physical health. If I were physically anemic I would never be able to escape pessimism. This very type of morbid introspection is one of the symptoms of the disease. I can't justify myself in my perilous position except by the observation that the business of being sophisticated and naive, critical and religious, at one and the same time is as difficult as it is necessary, and only a few are able to achieve the balance. H.—— says I lack a proper appreciation of the mystical values in religion. Yet I can't resist another word in self-defense. *The Modern world is so full of bunkum that it is difficult to attempt honesty in it without an undue emphasis upon the critical faculty.*[6]

The unease expressed by the young pastor in the face of his associate's piety could be a modern rendition, *mutatis mutandis*, of many things that Luther wrote in response to the apparently more secure faith of some of his associates, especially early in his career. What both the sixteenth century Reformer and the twentieth century American preacher were especially conscious of (and this will always distinguish such persons from the 'True Believers'!) was the undeniable reality of that which questions and threatens to negate belief, and the consequent difficulty of articulating one's faith without falling into more credulity and . . . 'bunkum'! To anticipate a little, I would posit that the psychological basis of Luther's *theologia crucis*, if it can be distinguished from its theoretical-doctrinal basis, is precisely his commitment to 'honest' reporting of what he finds in the world. Perhaps it was his peasant's incapacity for guile! 'The theology of glory', writes Luther in the 21st Thesis of his Heidelberg Disputation, 'has to call evil good and good evil, but the theology of the cross calls the thing what it really is'. Reinhold Niebuhr's 'Christian Realism' is surely rooted in this same psychic phenomenon. It is the product of a faith which has to survive, if it is to survive at all, within a spirit that is constitutionally incapable of spiritual-intellectual self-deception. Such a spirit is not necessarily reduced to cynicism because (as Niebuhr implies in the passage cited and states openly in many places) it is graciously enabled to see *behind* the crass and ambiguous realities of existence an ultimate meaning which both transcends and uses these realities. But it will not sacrifice its dogged 'honesty' about the world (say, the world of Henry Ford's assembly lines!) for the sake of achieving a more comfortable *personal* spirituality. It will not look *past* the Cross, but only *through* it. It will 'call the thing what it really is', even when that kind of intellectual rigour occasions such poignant *self*-criticism as can be heard in excerpts like the one just instanced.

For Niebuhr, however, this type of 'faithful realism' was if anything more painful than it was for Luther. For it is one thing to draw attention to that which negates in sixteenth century Europe, where few human beings in any case entertained very high expectations for life in this world; it is something else to do so in America during the first half of the twentieth century. Modern assumptions about history, as Niebuhr knew better than anyone, are notoriously expectant; and America was the place where it was all supposed to happen! What this means for *religion* in America is that it is under a permanent, generally unspoken but altogether effective obligation to provide the attitudinal undergirding that is essential to the psychic maintenance of 'The American Dream'.[7] For it is only in the last analysis a *religious* attitude – a credulity born of supra-rational conviction and continuously reaffirmed – that can achieve on the one hand the enthusiasm that is needed to 'buy into' the Dream and on the other the degree of repression required to avoid facing challenges to it. One reason why every form of religion is valued in American society, its real secularity notwithstanding, lies precisely within this socio-political imperative. Without so much as mentioning the differences between them, successive American presidents can laud religious leaders as divergent as Billy Graham and Norman Vincent Peale, Jerry Falwell and Robert Schuller. But by that same token there is one type of religious faith that the dominant culture will not tolerate; and that is a prophetic faith which out of a commitment to 'honesty' refuses *a priori* to contribute to the promotional and repressive functioning of the normative 'cultural religion'. Reinhold Niebuhr represented just such a faith.

Of course he might have pursued many of the

themes that he did pursue and, so to speak, without incident – sin, the tragic, irony, the ambiguity of human motives, the corruption of power, etc. – if only he had emphasized their resolution. Between the resurrectionism of the calvinistic tradition and the progressivism of an Enlightenment faith in which *Alles hat sich aufgeklärt* there are important ideational and practical differences. But what they have in common (and therefore they could achieve such a powerful mix in American history) is a penchant for resolution. Niebuhr resisted 'the pretension of finality'. Certainly he believed that whatever happened God would be 'with us'. But he never allowed this confidence of faith to be translated into ideological certitude, and he constantly warned that God's presence never ensures the triumph of our causes.

2. *The Logic of the Cross*

Though Martin Luther was a major contributor to one of the two incongruous accounts of the world between which he lived, Niebuhr was no 'Lutheran' in the conventional sense. He was particularly critical of the Saxon Reformer's ineptitude in the realm of social ethics and of the so-called 'Two Kingdoms Theory', which, in Niebuhr's earlier years at Union Seminary, was being hardened into dogma through the rationalizations of Erlangen and other theologians sympathetic to the Nazi enterprise. He was also of course dismayed, as most sensitive students of history have become, at the later Luther's blatant anti-Judaism. In general, Niebuhr deplored the fatalism by which Luther and his followers were perennially tempted, the point at which Luther's historical realism turned into resignation and *Weltschmerz*.

Yet Niebuhr's respect for Luther's basic approach to the Faith is undeniable. Luther, he wrote in his *magnum opus*, 'displays the most profound under-

standing of the meaning of Christian *agape*. . .';[8] and
in a later essay entitled simple, 'Germany', he speaks
of Luther's legacy as containing 'in my opinion . . . the
most profound religious insights on ultimate questions
of human existence. . .'.[9] Only Augustine, amongst historic theologians, plays a more conspicuous rôle than
Luther in Niebuhr's thought.[10]

As I have already intimated, I believe that what Professor Niebuhr gleaned from his life-long and varied
exposure to Luther was what is commonly referred to
as Luther's *theologia crucis.* So far as I am aware, Niebuhr has not used this technical term in any of his
writings; but the essential ingredients of this minority
tradition are all, as I shall attempt to show in the final
part of this statement, conspicuously present in his
work.

Before considering the elements of the tradition, it
would be useful to attempt a more general explication
of its character[11] – especially in an English-speaking
context where, as Ernst Käsemann has pointed out,[12]
the concept 'theology of the cross' is regularly heard
as if it referred narrowly to the doctrine of the atonement. What Luther intended by this term is certainly
not limited to soteriology. It refers to a whole
approach to the Faith – to a spirit and method per-
meating the entire theological enterprise. As a more
recent exponent of this tradition (Jürgen Moltmann)
has put it succinctly, '*Theologia crucis* is not a single
chapter in theology, but the key signature for all Christian theology.'[13]

No doubt Luther's own intuition was sound in that
when he first introduced the term (he did not *invent*
the tradition but only named it!) he immediately contrasted it with that other, broad theological convention
which in one form and another has dominated the
faith and doctrine of Christendom, named by Luther
theologia gloriae. More recent parlance designates it

'triumphalism'. The theology of the cross is at its core a *critical* theology, and the most common object of its critique is Christianity itself in its triumphalist expressions. It is therefore not at all accidental that all of those who have stood within this minority tradition – including Niebuhr – have been heard by their contemporaries chiefly as *critics*, and frequently chastised for it!

But while the theology of the cross is in some ways defined by its antithesis, it is not merely a critical theology. Even when historical circumstance requires of its advocates that they expend most of their creative energies criticizing the *status quo* (Kierkegaard!), the basic motivation of their critique is a highly definitive and even 'positive' understanding of the Gospel. Their castigation of triumphalism does not mean that they simply dispense with triumph. In a real sense, they are *preoccupied* with the triumph of divine grace, and particularly with a manner of conveying that triumph which does justice to its profundity and avoids the (almost unavoidable!) suggestion of so much Christianity that 'Easter' is a too easy, theoretical resolution of the human predicament. Instead of embracing an evangelical formula in which the resurrection supersedes the cross, therefore, the advocates of this tradition locate the mystery of the divine *agape* in the cross. The cross remains the fundamental statement both of the human condition and of the divine redemption. The function of the resurrection is that it 'establishes Christ's cross as a saving event'.[14] Thus what the triumphalist mentality identifies as the negative, dark and therefore at most the *pen*ultimate point of the Christian story ('Black Friday'!) is itself already astonishingly positive. *Omnia bona in cruce et sub cruce abscondita sunt* (Luther): everything *good* is already there – but 'hidden beneath its opposite' and therefore accessible only to faith. That is to say, *in*accessible to the kind of mentality that thinks of belief in terms of possessing rather than hoping, that wants to have arrived instead of being *en route*, that looks to transcendent grace for a way out of the world with its doubts and ambiguities instead of a way into it.

The cross of Jesus Christ is the paradigmatic centre of this whole mode of thought – and of course it is more than a mere paradigm. Yet it is not to be made so unique and discontinuous with every other moment in history that it loses its capacity to embody and address the human situation. It is paradigmatic in that it illuminates every other event, and the whole course of history. The problematique to which it speaks is a human one, and one of which all human beings have some awareness: How are we to live knowing that we die? – a question which, as Niebuhr frequently pointed out, is not merely about the problem of our morality (the question which preoccupied the Greek mind) but about the *meaning* of our mortal life. In the face of all that negates 'life' in the broadest biblical sense of the term, how are we to find 'the courage to be' (Tillich)? Are we to become in that well-known sense 'religious' and nurture some 'illusion' (Freud) which offers us a triumphal world *view* at the expense of honesty about the real *world*? Or are we (as Ernest Becker said of Freud himself) to relinquish in the name of intellectual honesty every sort of capacity for hope, every insistence of the human spirit that truth may be more mysterious and 'user friendly' than our most scientific observations of it?[15] Hans Küng has said, insightfully, that 'Coping with the negative side of life is the acid test of Christian faith and non-Christian humanisms.'[16] Cynical realism capitulates to the negative side. Religious and secular ideologies of triumph create simplistic or complicated theoretical victories over it. The 'logic of the cross' (Niebuhr's own term) is impelled by the conviction that to abandon the earnest contemplation, analysis and transformation of the negative is to abandon humanity, and by the hope (hope against hope!) that *the negative side itself*, as with Christ's cross, already conceals a strangely positive *telos*: that life can be entered only through a heightened encounter with death, that hope is real only when it emerges 'on the far side of despair' (Keats), that faith comes to be only in the struggle with existential doubt, that the City of God must be sought for in the ruins of the human city.

It is this cruciform 'logic' that informs every major theo-historical judgement of Reinhold Niebuhr. He knew himself to be part of a society that had been *victimized* by a 'theology of glory' which required it to be oblivious of its own guilt and failures and, since it was also very powerful, an increasing danger within the community of nations. He believed that the only salvation for such a society was to discover a vantage-point from which to expose itself to its own inordinate pride and folly but without capitulating to the kind of despair which leads to nihilism and thus by another route to annihilation. For Niebuhr, it could be said, the whole weight of biblical faith was directed precisely towards the gaining of such a perspective: 'It envisages antinomies, contradictions and tragic realities within the framework [of meaning] without succumbing to despair.'[17] The Gospel of the Cross was almost designed for such a context as ours: having 'lived through . . . centuries of hope' which 'have well nigh destroyed the Christian faith as a potent force in modern culture and civilization,' we find ourselves now in one of those 'periods of disillusionment when the vanity of such hopes is fully revealed'. This does not ensure that the Christian faith will be restored; 'It has merely re-established its relevance' – namely the relevance of a system of belief that is able 'to find life meaningful without placing an abortive confidence in

. . . mere historical growth'.[18] Christianity can lay claim to this relevance, not by attempting a return to the 'Age of Belief', but by achieving a 'new synthesis' in which the insights of biblical religion are combined with aspects of the Reformation and Renaissance to give a vision in which, on the one hand, 'life in history must be recognized as filled with indeterminate possibilities', and on the other hand 'that every effort and pretension to complete life, whether in collective or individual terms, that every desire to stand beyond the contradictions of history, or to eliminate the final corruptions of history must be disavowed.'[19]

Thus from the vantage-point of the Cross, faith is enabled to contemplate failure without either courting it fatalistically or being reduced to despair by its prospect. As a civilization, Niebuhr thought, we do not know whether we are about to collapse or whether we are about to open into a new dimension of 'world community':

> Standing inside such a civilization our responsibilities are obvious: We must seek to fashion our common life to conform more nearly to the brotherhood of the Kingdom of God. No view of history *sub specie aeternitatis* dare beguile us from our historical obligations. But if we should fail, as well we may, we can at least understand the failure from the perspective of the Christian faith. Insofar as we understand the failure we will not be completely involved in it, but have a vantage point beyond it. We could not deny the tragic character of what we discern but we would not be tempted to regard it as meaningless.[20]

It would be hard to find a more faithful translation into contemporary socio-historical terms of the *theologia crucis*.

3. Ingredients of the Tradition

The theology of the cross, I have insisted, implies an entire mode of thinking the Faith. No brief account of any of its exemplars can exhaust the meaning of this tradition; but for the sake of concreteness we may consider briefly four characteristic features of the tradition and Niebuhr's handling of them:

(a) *The Epistemological Dimension:* The *theologia crucis* is first of all a theology of *faith.*[21] The *sola fide* of the Reformation is deeply present in Niebuhr's thought.[22] While he rejected the fide*ism* of the Barthian school[23], he was critical of hellenistic and modern expressions of belief because of their tendency 'to transmute into truths of speculative reason' what can only be received by faith and expressed symbolically.[24] 'The truth which is revealed in the cross is not a truth which could have been anticipated in human culture and it is not the culmination of human wisdom.'[25]

Niebuhr's struggle in this respect, however, is not merely the continuing battle of Reformation Christianity against other historical forms of the Faith. It is the intensely practical struggle of a North American who finds himself the inheritor of a tradition in which faith implies an ongoing dialogue with doubt (Luther's *Anfechtungen!*) in the midst of a religious community where belief seems to involve no existential struggle. Niebuhr did not find belief *easy!* Over against the American-style *theologia gloriae* which goes beyond the medieval rational acceptance of God to a faith-posture which hardly even has to think in order to 'believe', Niebuhr's consciousness of 'the foolishness of the cross' stands out in sharp contrast. Faith is faith, not sight! 'True religion must therefore be conscious of the difficulty and the absurdity of the human claiming kinship with the divine, of the temporal trafficking with the eternal. If the divine is made relevant to the human, it must transvalue our values and enter the human at the point where man is lowly rather than proud and where he is weak rather than strong.'[26] Such a statement, very typical of Niebuhr, mirrors many of Luther's; but it also goes beyond Luther because it assumes the characteristic twentieth century experience of 'the Absurd', and challenges Christians to think the faith within the context of what Niebuhr's friend, W.H. Auden, named 'The Age of Anxiety'.

(b) *The Ontological Dimension:* The basic ontological assumption of the theology of the cross might be stated in some such way as this: that the relation between the experienced reality we call Nature and the experienced reality we call Grace is a dialectical one, in which the dimensions of continuity and discontinuity are in constant tension. The most characteristic disagreement between Niebuhr and his long-time colleague, Paul Tillich, was that Niebuhr felt Tillich accentuated too consistently the dimension of continuity. He distrusted Tillich's whole 'ontological' approach to Christian faith because of its inherent propensity to blur the distinction between Creator and Creation and thus to minimize both the reality of creaturely freedom and the radicality of divine grace.[27] 'Protestant theology is right in setting grace in contradiction to nature in the sense that the vicious circle of false truth, apprehended from the standpoint of the self, must be broken and the self cannot break it. In that sense the apprehension of the truth in Christ is always a miracle; and "flesh and blood have not revealed it unto us".'[28]

At the same time, an undialectical emphasis upon discontinuity, while it may be desirable strategically under certain circumstances (as at Barmen in 1934), introduces the phenomenon of a God whose being and acting touches human historical existence not at all. Thus in the famous debate between Barth and Brunner, culminating in Barth's angry response, *Nein!*, Niebuhr's sympathies lay with Brunner. '. . . Protestant theology . . . is wrong in denying the "point of contact" (*Anknüpfungspunkt*) which always exists in man by virtue of the residual element of *justitia originalis* in his being.'[29]

Yet while the historic debate between the two Swiss theologians issued in a redefining of 'Orthodoxy' (Neo-Orthodoxy) that eventually incorporated many beyond Europe's boundaries, this was not the matrix in which Niebuhr's working-out of the relation between nature and grace occurred. Again we are reminded that, for him, the Reformation tradition had to express itself in a specifically 'New World' context; and the temptation of Christianity in that context, while it was certainly also connected with a one-sided emphasis on the continuity factor, did not attach itself as in Europe to a political ideology which used 'Natural Theology' to undergird its racial and other theories, but was associated with theological Liberalism's tendency to sentimentalize the Gospel and thus eliminate the critical side of theology. In his preaching and other theological work, therefore, Niebuhr found it necessary again and again to draw attention to the 'otherness' of the reality introduced by grace. It was this necessity which, I believe, caused the theological community to begin to regard him as an exponent of Neo-Orthodoxy – though he in fact differed significantly from the trends of this movement.[30] Reinhold Niebuhr could not have written Karl Barth's essay about 'The Strange New World Within the Bible';[31] but his consciousness of Modernity's elevation of human being and of the modern Church's accommodation to that elevation made him all the same a strong spokesperson in the American scene for the ontic 'distance between the human the divine.'[32] While grace does in fact meet and perfect nature, there is for this tradition no faithful experience of that grace which escapes the *skandalon* of its mode of engaging the world.[33]

(c) *The Soteriological Dimension:* The difference between *theologia gloriae* and *theologia crucis* is the difference between salvation as resolution and salvation as engagement. A theological triumphalism which posits salvation as a *fait accompli* does not *necessarily* preclude ethics; it may produce a perfectionist ethic or an ethical passivity, depending upon whether its orientation is towards this world or 'the next'. But salvation interpreted as the dynamic influence of grace in the ongoing struggles of history leads necessarily to an ethic that is not merely consequential but an integral dimension of the core of the Gospel itself.

A very good case could be made, I think, for claiming that Reinhold Niebuhr was driven to his abiding vocational concern for Christian ethics because his understanding of the nature of salvation was what it was. Niebuhr understood the work of God in Christ as God's decisive participation in the historical process. This is not however the participation of a divine omnipotence which sets aside every obstacle. It is the participation of a suffering love which alters the world, not through power but through solidarity with suffering humanity: 'The suffering servant does not impose goodness upon the world by his power. Rather, he suffers, being powerless, from the injustices of the powerful. He suffers most particularly from the sins of the righteous who do not understand how full of unrighteousness is all human righteousness.'[34]

While ethical obedience is thus an aspect of soteriology for Niebuhr, it is not however a lapse into 'works righteousness' – for Niebuhr any more than for Bonhoeffer. Niebuhr had an inate appreciation for

Luther's *simul justus et peccator* which is perhaps unparalleled in the New World! It made him very impatient with Christian perfectionists, 'who still do not understand the logic of the Cross. They hope that if goodness is only perfect enough its triumph in history will be assured.'[35]

(d) *The Eschatological Dimension:* The theology of the cross sustains two difficult orientations simultaneously: a determination to be entirely 'realistic' about evil in the world, and the insistence that historical existence is meaningful. Such a tradition will always be at odds therefore with two alternatives, both of them products of the triumphalist impulse: on the one hand it will reject the world view which posits a too easy triumph of the good in history; on the other it will reject the more characteristically 'religious' option which abandons history in favour of a supramundane *denouement.*

Not surprisingly then, Niebuhr found himself doing frequent battle on two fronts. The Christian Gospel '. . . implies a refutation . . . of both utopianism and a too consistent otherworldliness. Against utopianism the Christian faith insists that the final consummation of history lies beyond the conditions of the temporal process. Against otherworldliness it asserts that the consummation fulfils rather than negates the historical process.'[36] Both these temptations were strongly present in Niebuhr's context, but because his *formative* experience belonged to the *first* half of this century it was the danger of triumphalistic religious and secular utopianism that preoccupied him, understandably enough. He was conscious in particular of the sin of optimism: 'Faith is always imperilled on the one side by despair and on the other side by optimism. Of these two enemies of faith, optimism is the more dangerous.'[37]

Whoever listens today to the pronouncements of the official optimists of our technocracy will sympathize! But for us who have survived into the *last* half of 'The Christian Century' (!), there is a new awareness of the hollowness of this optimism. It is precisely . . . 'official!' That is, it cloaks a public cynicism – a covert nihilism perhaps – whose only trust is in arms, not in history or God. Or if in God, then in a God who is preparing to abandon the world – therefore not the God of Golgotha! Niebuhr was too sensitive a student of humanity not to notice the emergence of this new barbarism, and therefore he warned Christians against the final temptation – what Bonhoeffer rightly identified as the temptation 'to write this world off prematurely'.[38] I suspect that it is *this* side of the eschatology of the Cross that Christians and all persons of goodwill shall have to concentrate upon from now on; for while 'The Christian faith in the goodness of God is not to be equated with a confidence in the virtue of man. . . .

> . . . neither is it a supernaturalism and otherworldliness which places its hope in another world because it finds this world evil. Every distinction between an essentially good eternity and an essentially evil finiteness is foreign to the Christian faith. When Christians express their faith in such terms they have been corrupted by other types of religion. For the Christian who really understands his faith, life is worth living and this world is not merely "a vale of tears". He is able to discern the goodness of creation beneath the corruptions of human sin. . . . He will not suffer the tortures of the cynics who falsely equate their ideals with their achievements and regard their fellow men with bitterness because the latter fail to measure up to their ideals.[39]

There is no facile way for humankind to achieve the future. 'The Kingdom of God must still enter the

world by way of crucifixion.'[40] But it is the world that
God's Kingdom enters, and for Christians to abandon
this world is to abandon the Cross at its centre.

NOTES

1. Niebuhr's denominational background must be traced to the 'Church
of the Prussian Union' (Deutsche Evangelische Kirchenverein des
Westens), which was a union superimposed upon the Lutheran and
Reformed churches of Prussia on the 300th anniversary of the Reformation by King Frederick William III in 1817. Gustav Niebuhr, Reinhold's
father, grew up within this tradition, and was himself one of its shapers
in the American scene. As John C. Bennett has rightly observed, therefore, 'Luther was an important influence in [Niebuhr] denomination
but it was not confessionally Lutheran. This explains his emphasis on
Luther and the freedom with which he approached Luther.' (Wm. G.
Chrystal, Ed., *Young Reinhold Niebuhr: His Early Writings*, St. Louis,
Eden Publishing House, 1977; p. 13).

2. *Cf.* e.g. *The Irony of American History:* 'It is particularly remarkable
that the two great religious-moral traditions which informed our early
life – New England Calvinism and Virginian Deism and Jeffersonianism
– arrive at remarkably similar conclusions about the meaning of our
national character and destiny. Calvinism may have held too pessimistic views of human nature, and too mechanical views of the providen-
tial ordering of human life. But when it assessed the significance of
the American experiment both its conceptions of American destiny and
its appreciation of American virtue finally arrived at conclusions strik-
ingly similar to those of Deism. Whether our nation interprets its spiritual heritage through Massachusetts or Virginia, we came into existence
with the sense of being a 'separated' nation, which God was using to
make a new beginning for mankind. . . . Whether, as in the case of the
New England theocrats, our forefathers thought of our 'experiment' as
primarily the creation of a new and purer church, or, as in the case of
Jefferson and his coterie they thought primarily of a new political
community, they believed in either case that we had been called out
by God to create a new humanity. We were God's "American Israel".'
(pp. 23–24).

3. 'If one were to compute [a percentage of Calvinist heritage] on the
basis of all the German, Swiss, French, Dutch and Scottish people
whose forebears bore the "stamp of Geneva" in some broader sense,
85 or 90 percent would not be an extravagant estimate.' Sydney E.
Ahlstrom on the influence of Calvinism in the USA, in *A Religious
History of the American People*, Vol. I (Garden City, N.Y, Doubleday &
Co. Inc. (Image Books), 1975); p. 169. See also Sydney E. Mead, *The
Lively Experiment: The Shaping of Christianity in America* (New York,
Harper & Row Publishers, 1963), pp. 142 f.

4. *The Nature and Destiny of Man*, Vol. II, p. 185.
5. Even today it is hard to find Christian scholars who regard Niebuhr as a *theologian*. Categorizing him as 'a Christian ethicist', while it may be accurate enough in certain respects, is frequently a cloaked way of discounting him as an interpreter of the Faith as a whole. Certainly he was not a *systematic* theologian, and he did not aspire to be such. But then, neither was Martin Luther! A notable exception to this generalization is George A. Lindbeck, who in his recent study, *The Nature of Doctrine: Religion and Theology in a Postliberal Age* (Philadelphia, The Westminster Press, 1984; p.124) writes: 'Perhaps the last American theologian who in practice (and in some extent in theory) made extended and effective attempts to redescribe major aspects of the contemporary scene in distinctively Christian terms was Reinhold Niebuhr.'
6. New York, Richard R. Smith, Inc., 1930; p. 132-133.
7. This is not so dominant in Canada, where we possess only a 'pale version' of the American Dream, and where both political and geographic realities thrust us into a struggle for survival that is not so conducive to credulity and indeed breeds a scepticism that is not always amenable to 'religion'.
8. *The Nature and Destiny of Man*, Vol. II, *op.cit.*, p. 187.
9. *Worldview*, June, 1973; p. 14.
10. Responding to Richard Kroner's analysis of 'The Historical Roots of Niebuhr's Thought' (in Charles W. Kegley and Robert W. Bretall, Eds., *Reinhold Niebuhr: His Religious, Social and Political Thought* (N.Y., The Macmillan Co, 1956)), Niebuhr writes, 'In regard to Professor Kroner's sympathetic account of the movement of my thought, I have only a slight amendment to suggest, and that is that I was first influenced not so much by the Reformers as by the study of St. Augustine.' (pp. 436-37). One may be permitted to ask, however, and especially in view of the significant differences between Protestant and Catholic analyses of Augustine, whether Niebuhr's Augustine is not rather coloured by Protestant associations!
11. I have discussed this tradition in numerous writings, especially *Lighten Our Darkness: Towards an Indigenous Theology of the Cross* (Philadelphia, The Westminster Press, 1976), where I have also acknowledged my indebtedness to my great teacher, Niebuhr, for his exemplary treatment of the tradition in the North American context.
12. 'The Pauline Theology of the Cross', in *Interpretation*, Vol. XXIV, No. 2, April, 1970; p. 227.
13. *The Crucified God* (London, SCM Press, Ltd., 1973); p. 72. Jürgen Moltmann.
14. *Theology of Play*, trans. by Reinhard Ulrich (N.Y., Harper & Row, 1972), p. 30.
15. See Ernest Becker, *The Denial of Death* (N.Y., The Free Press, 1973).
16. *On Being a Christian*, trans. by Edward Quinn (Glasgow, Collins, 1974); p. 571.
17. *Faith and History: A Comparison of Christian and Modern Views of History*, pp. 28-29.

18. *The Nature and Destiny of Man*, Vol. II, *op.cit.*, pp. 206–207.
19. *Ibid.*, p. 207.
20. *Ibid.*, p. 308.
21. See Walther von Loewenich, *Luther's Theology of the Cross*, trans. by Herbert J. A. Bouman (Belfast, Christian Journals Ltd., 1976); Chapter II.
22. 'The correlate of revelation is faith. The mutual relation between the two is so close that revelation cannot be completed without faith. The revelation of God in Christ, the disclosure of God's sovereignty over life and history, the clarification of the meaning of life and history, is not completed until man is able, by faith, to apprehend the truth which is beyond his apprehension without faith.' (*The Nature and Destiny of Man*, Vol. II, p. 52).
23. 'The truth is not *completely* beyond [human] apprehension; otherwise Christ could not have been expected. It *is* nevertheless beyond his apprehension, or Christ would not have been rejected. It is a truth capable of apprehension by faith; but when so apprehended there is a consciousness in the heart of the believer that he has been helped to this apprehension.' (*Ibid*)
24. *Ibid.*, p. 60.
25. *Ibid.*, p. 62.
26. *The Christian Century*, vol. 100, October 12, 1983; pp. 900–901.
27. See 'Biblical Thought and Ontological Speculation in Tillich's Theology', by Reinhold Niebuhr, in Charles W. Kegley and Robert W. Bretall, *The Theology of Paul Tillich* (N.Y., The Macmillan Co, 1952); pp. 216 ff.
28. *The Nature and Destiny of Man*, vol. II, *op.cit.*, p. 64.
29. In his footnote to this sentence, Niebuhr writes: 'In this debate Brunner seems to me to be right and Barth wrong; but Barth seems to win the debate because Brunner accepts too many of Barth's presuppositions in his fundamental premises to be able to present his own position with plausibility and consistency. Barth is able to prove Brunner inconsistent, but that does not necessarily prove him to be wrong.' (*Ibid.*)
30. The foregoing footnote is typical of Niebuhr's distancing of himself even from the Brunnerian articulation of this movement.
31. In Karl Barth, *The Word of God and the Word of Man* (N.Y., Harper & Bros., Harper Torchbooks, 1957).
32. 'When the Word was made flesh it not only revealed the relevance between the human and the divine but the distance between the human and the divine.' (*The Christian Century*, vol. 100, *op.cit.*)
33. 'To recognize that the Cross was something more than a noble tragedy and its victim something else than a good man who died for his ideals; to behold rather that this suffering was indicative of God's triumph over evil through a love which did not stop at involvement in the evil over which it triumphed; to see, in other words, the whole mystery of God's mercy disclosed here is to know that the crucified Lord had triumphed over death and "when he had himself purged our sins, sat down on the right hand of the Majesty on High" (Hebrews 1:3)'. (*Faith and History, op.cit.*, p. 147.)

34. *Beyond Tragedy: Essays on the Christian Interpretation of History*, p. 181.
35. *Faith and History, op.cit.*, p. 128.
36. *Beyond Tragedy, op.cit.*, p. 175.
37. *Ibid.*, p. 115.
38. *Letters and Papers from Prison* (London, SCM Press, 1971); p. 336 f.
39. *Beyond Tragedy, op.cit.*, p. 132.
40. *Ibid.*, p. 185.

LIST OF WRITINGS

The following major writings of Niebuhr are referred to in the text by their title only.

Leaves from the Notebook of a Tamed Cynic, Chicago 1929, reissued NY 1957

Moral Man and Immoral Society, Charles Scribner's, NY 1932

Reflections on the End of an Era, Charles Scribner's, NY 1932

An Interpretation of Christian Ethics, Harper and Brothers, NY 1935, paperback edition 1979, Seabury

Beyond Tragedy: Essays on the Christian Interpretation of History, Charles Scribner's, 1937. Reissued 1965.

Christianity and Power Politics, Charles Scribner's, NY 1940, reprinted 1969

The Nature and Destiny of Man: A Christian Interpretation, Vol. I *Human Nature*, Charles Scribner's, NY 1941. Vol. II *Human Destiny*, Charles Scribner's, NY 1943. Reissued 1964

The Children of Light and the Children of Darkness, 1945

The Irony of American History, Charles Scribner's, NY 1952

Christian Realism and Political Problems, Charles Scribner's, NY and Faber, London 1953

Faith and History: A Comparison of Christian and Modern Views of History, Charles Scribner's, NY 1959

Man's Nature and His Communities, Charles Scribner's, NY 1965